13

LOS ANGELES

POETS

The ONTHEBUS Poets Series

Number One

Edited by Jack Grapes

Bombshelter Press
Los Angeles, 1997

Library of Congress Catalog Number: 95-83261

ISBN 0-941017-47-X

Some of the poems in this book have previously appeared in the following publications: ONTHEBUS, *Voices, onTarget, Blood Pudding, Northstone Review, Metizta, Pearl, Northwest, Rattle, Spillway, Myriad, Exquisite Corpse, Sycamore Review, Poetry East, Wormwood Review, Cybrocal, Verve, Red Dance Floor, Tsunami, Sheila-Na-Gig, Rohwedder, Cold Drill, West/Word, Mosaic, Second Glance, Electrum, Poetry LA, Vol.No., Whoreson Dog*; and the following anthologies: *News From Inside, Truth and Lies That Press for Life, Women and Death, Voices* (Israel), and *The New Los Angeles Poets*.

Bombshelter Press
P.O. Box 481266
Bicentennial Station
Los Angeles, CA 90048

Cover design by Judith James.
Cover photograph by permission from Univeral Studios.
All photographs were take by Lisa Cricks, except Jan Ruckerts' by David Weininger and Stellasue Lee's by Toby Near.

13 Los Angeles Poets

KATHLEEN ZEISLER GOLDMAN

KATHLEEN ZEISLER GOLDMAN lives in Mahhattan Beach with her husband and children. A journalist by training, after her children were born she found herself working at a pre-school for eight years. More recently she has taught creative writing to elementary school children and adults. She aspires to return to journalism as a science columnist. Her poems have appeared in *Northeast, ONTHEBUS, Pearl, Spillway* and *Myriad.*

THIS TIME OF YEAR

Mother died in January,
sometime around now, I think—in the 20s.
This is the first year I haven't gone a little nuts
until I realized, "Oh, Mother died in January."
Maybe it's because this year I didn't forget,
so that my craziness had to remind me,
"You are sad."
This loss of Mother, I was so young,
but I am not young anymore.
I feel the weight of should: I should be over it.
She died a long time ago.
I should be grown up by now, not wishing
I could have one more conversation with her.
Not wishing I could introduce her to Neil and the kids.
She would like them so much.
They are as beautiful as her own babies,
all blond and big brown eyes,
all sturdy legs and energy. She would like them.
And I should be over it.

THE SUNDAY SOCCER GAME

The never-get-it mutter on my shoulder. Parrot-mutter
on my shoulder. Bright colors—yellow, oranges, reds, greens—
mostly green as the grass underfoot. Little girls run
red-faced, fall side-ached on the field I cannot touch
for lack of hearing, "Run as fast as you can,"
on fields and roads, on pathways
out among the poplar, birch and elm,
the oak and maple torched by autumn air and sunshine
to the parrot colors, less the green.
Every path leads inward from the center,
a sort of earthy dark matter spins me counterclockwise
straight down to the mid-section tumble of light
and dark, of sun hard on the heels of shadow.
Shadow wins, and I am lost

in that world of dappled light deep in woods
where leaves drop to the mutter of my mother's rosary,
her mumbled darkness next to mine.

CLEANING DAY

The house busy with clean,
loud machine clean,
all new.
Mary cannot focus, wants to follow,
wants to direct, wants to wave bye-bye,
wants to remember where has Daddy gone.

Mary wants to remember
all her children—all five—
Richard, Michael, James, Anne, Kathleen,
but she draws a blank after four.
After Anne comes no name.

Clairvoyant says I know,
but who cares?
Knowing means nothing.
Knowing remembers.
Knowing can't forget
the way Mary forgot.

Mary calls her sister Lucille
and says she has forgotten when is dinner time.
When is it time to put on the meat,
peel the potatoes,
wash the vegetables.
And who is the strange girl
who comes from school,
says, "Hi, Mom. I'm home."

All is forgotten, the first sight,
second, third, fourth,

every year a new sight
and still no change.

Mary hides her money
for fear the stranger in her house
will steal it and more—
her wedding china, pots and pans,
the iron,
photos of her mother, Agnes.
The schoolgirl looks like Agnes,
but, most days,
Mary remembers Agnes is dead.

As for me, my vision grows dimmer
every year.
Like Mary, I cannot focus and wave bye-bye.
Like Mary, I smile mouth smiles.
Hand drops, hand waits;
eyes look and cannot focus.
Eyes look and cannot focus.

DOWN RIVER

Music piped into the patisserie
helps me digest cranberry lemon lane tea,
my stomach no longer empty,
me no longer angry, growling
at the threat of rain
already puddled, reflecting the sky.
Birds fluff fat
in order to stay dry
and the fat and the thin
wander this city built
where rain has always been infrequent.
We thumb our noses at drought,
seek coca extracts, poppy brews,
expect showers of flowers

palmed sinister
in left hands and never mind
the cost in lives
north and south and south.
The fanfare anticipates the horns
undermining cornet.
Somewhere dirt floors sweep clean.
I wish for dark
where monster Caliban feels free to rape,
and chocolate croissants
in sombrero shapes
belie the muddle of language.

This is a dangerous place.
The loaves packed
against the wall remind me of logs
packed tight into rafts—my river days.
The current dragging
bodies to shore
bloated and waiting
for Mama to arrive,
to identify me,
to recognize the shape
she cradled. I still fit
into the crook of her arm
if she can stand the stink
of days' old death.
I am her lovely child.
Once her fingers
encircled my wrist.
My mouth tugged
her breast.
These putrid lips
smiled just for her.
My rotting eyes
saw only her.
She counted my fingers and toes.
She counted me,
her fifth child,
the baby.

COOL IRON IF NECESSARY

Gold melts down
past liquid meant
to test our mettle,
meant to tell us
who and what and who
and who

who slouches toward Bethlehem.
And where, I ask aloud,
is God this Sunday
dawn? Drawn
to baptism by immersion

as if souls get clean
under water.
Pour in detergent
one cup at a time.
Do not overfill.
Rinse thoroughly.
Dry medium. Cool iron.

WEST WIND

Nothing beautiful here, not like
the Bishop—the sign of the fish
through holes cut in thin ice.

No one can remember a January
as cold as the one
when Mother died.

Or a March as warm as when Daddy did.
Hot west wind past windows open
to a lawn gone green too soon.

Give me July when I was born,
any season
when no one dies.

A BLESSING ON SPIDERS
AND OTHER LIVING THINGS

I am in the family room.
Sphinx is having his usual late-morning-early-afternoon nap.
I will not write about how Anne viewed Mother,
or how Zeke viewed Mother,
or how Mike or Jim or Aunt Ceil viewed Mother.
I will not write about how Daddy viewed her,
either when he was alive or after he was dead.
I will not write about how they viewed Kathy,
the one child still dependent on Mother,
crazy, crazy Mother.
Instead, I will write about the new denim cushions on my couch,
the geometric Mexican Indian patterns on the rug,
the weak shaft of sunlight through the south window,
the window that looks out onto my backyard.

There is a spider web in the east corner
of the south window.
I have knocked that web down over and over.
I have tried to catch the spider that weaves it,
to put her outside in the garden
where I tell her there will be more for her to eat.
But she eludes me. She gets down into the crack of the window
where the side that opens slides onto the side that doesn't,
and she disappears.
Maybe she will find her own way to the garden.
After all, she found her own way into the house.
The next day, or the day after that,
I look, and there is the web again,
reminding me for all the world

of a big clot of dust, only prettier,
wispier, up where it connects to the window sill.

Last year Micah and his friend Matt found a spider egg sac
in a similar spot on the living room window.
They experimented by opening it up,
and out came hundreds of baby spiders.
"Mom," he said, "on accident, Matt let some spiders out
in the living room."
I went down, and there they were—
kind of cute, but way too many to just let free in the house,
and I couldn't catch them all and put them outside,
so I got a damp paper towel and wiped them up.
I felt bad.
They had all eight of their legs.
They had their sectioned bodies.
And besides, spiders are good to have in the yard.
So I told Micah that if he ever finds another spider egg sac,
to take it outside so the spiders will be born
where they can live and eat each other and the bugs
that aren't good for the yard.

This, my feeble attempt to respect nature.
I try. I, who live in a gas-heated house
of cut trees and mixed concrete,
a house with hot and cold running water
sucked from under Kern County.
I, who drive a car that runs on processed dinosaurs.
I, who eat foods from the supermarket,
grown on ground saturated with herbicides and pesticides
and wear synthetic clothing
and natural fiber clothing grown like my food,
I try. I recycle into the big white smoke-belching truck.
I plant my yard in drought-friendly plants.
I nurture my sick eucalyptus tree.
I, who take long, hot baths and dye my hair, I try.
I put spiders outside and bless them on their way.

THIS KNIT AND PURL OF PASTS

I got lost driving back from Minneapolis
to my hometown just ninety miles south and east
across the Mississippi River in Wisconsin.
I got lost driving through a real Midwestern rainstorm
and the green hills and fields and trees.
I looked at cornfields, sky-high and lush.
When I was little my brothers and sister and I
played hide-and-seek in the field near our grandfather's house.
This looked like home, and you don't get lost at home.

Lightning darts in the sky.
I have seen the way its tongue
licks the trees, splitting them.
I am warm in its glow like in a wool sweater.
I am comfortable in it like the gouges
in Mother's dining room table,
black in the ancient oak,
the color of coffee before cream.

When I was a child, Mother bought me purple flowers.
She said they were my treat,
would last through thick air.
This is my memory here among memories.
I can choose the finest and burn the rest.
It is my gift. It rides in my chest
like the flurry of green leaves
in ancient elms when the wind comes up.
It stays in my hearing
like morning doves, like robins,
like the rain on the roof.
Somehow I turned onto a county road—Alt Truck Rte 90.
It was absolutely dark, no farm houses, just fields
and my kids saying where are we?
In L.A. I study my maps as a hedge against getting lost.
I always know when I have taken a wrong turn.
I plan my own alternate routes.
Here at home I can't be the mommy.

I can't tell my children where we are.
Here at home I am afraid of losing us altogether.

SOME OTHER ALICE, SOME OTHER LAND

This morning I walked along the road
past fields of corn on one side
and soybeans on the other.
There was an abandoned farm house
next to a ramshackle barn with cattle inside.

I am this place, long grass,
flat prairie and distant hills.
The wind is cold in January
when the fields are bare, but in August,
ripening crops and heat shimmers
fill the space from river to bluff to eye.

I am the marten
that catches bugs in flight,
that weaves her nest
of long, stray grass,
the mown hay across the road.
I am all this and a storm
of red-winged blackbirds
scared out by the harvester.
I know what a windrow is—I have seen one
neatly laid out in anticipation.

I doze here in the dark tunnel
made by full-grown corn,
tall enough to hide the magic from the magician,
large enough to see the sunflowers
at the borders of the field.

A WOMAN'S PLACE

I am fat,
a chocolate mousse,
a whipped-cream confection,
but I am also as dense as hand weights,
as the barbell across my shoulders—
the barbell designed
and manufactured by men.
I am a woman,
my mother's fragile child,
Mary's little lamb
who rarely chooses what to do.
O, the weight of it.
My little arms will break,
my ribs crush and pierce my lung,
the left one, the one adjacent to my heart.

I cannot live here
in this place of strong
anymore than I can live
in that other place of smart.
I do better in the kitchen,
preparing salad, homemade sauces, tomato puree,
slicing meat from bones,
my pink chicken flesh, my red beef flesh,
my somewhere-in-between of turkey, pork and veal flesh.
Never lamb.
I do not like it well enough to pay the price.
The price, always exhorbitant, chatters at me
through the glass at the meat counter,
"I am too much. You cannot.
You cannot, you cannot, you cannot, you cannot,
you cannot."

MY LIFE'S WORK

My cranium is so full,
some days I need a diuretic
so I can see the trees in my own yard
and hear the birds, the traffic sounds.
My eyes and ears clog up
so I can only hear and rehear my husband
telling me how we must economize.
"It's all so simple," he says.
"You will clean the house.
You will cook the meals.
You will do the laundry,
tend the children,
and get a job—one that pays this time."

My poems are written on toilet paper,
functional yet temporary,
soon out to sea to choke
marine mammals, to dull sharks' teeth
and to pollute *Beach Blanket Bingo*.
Annette and Frankie sent me a bottle
of invisible ink
with a note attached: "Drink me."

I drank it.
So now I weigh the pros and cons,
and drink some more.
The only side-effect is odd—I think I am here,
only I can't see me.
All my mirrors have gone black.
But I can honestly say my writing has improved.
I can honestly say he is right,
it is all so simple.
I can honestly say,
this is a lie everyone can spot.
Except me.

STEPHANIE HAGER

STEPHANIE HAGER grew up in San Diego and received a B.A. in sociology from Pomona College in 1990. She has lived in Los Angeles for seven years and recently completed a master's program in social work at UCLA. Her poems have been published in numerous magazines across the country, including *Exquisite Corpse, Sycamore Review, Poetry East, Wormwood Review* and *ONTHEBUS*. She is looking for a publisher for her first full-length manuscript, *My Long-Spent Body.*

THE GIVING OF WORDS

All of a sudden, I think of Abraham
the other morning when he ran out
into the main living room wearing all red—
red t-shirt, red sweatpants—
and started running around one of the red tables
with that crazy look on his face
saying, "I'm the devil. I'm the devil."
And without even thinking, I said,
"No you're not. You're a big red valentine heart."
He kept running around in that circle
and saying, "I'm the devil." So I said it again,
"You're a big red valentine heart.
Now take these socks and go back down to your room.
Bye-bye, Mr. Valentine."
And that's what I called him
the rest of the morning. Mr. Valentine.
And he did too. Mr. Valentine. Mr. Valentine Heart.

I think I would like to be able
to ask for help so plainly and get it.
If I lost my voice tomorrow
I would have better relationships with everyone I know
because I wouldn't have to worry
about saying anything anymore. I would just write.
Two nights ago, I was sitting at my computer
and the phone rang and it was Mike,
so right away I figure he wants to come down
and spend the night, but we talk.
And pretty soon we're talking about
how I can't talk about things
and he says it takes practice,
I should practice with him. And I say, "I know.
I always mean to but I don't." He says, "O.K.
Do you want me to come down there?"
I say, "Yeah." So he says, "So say
'Mike, I want you to come down
and we'll do what we did the other night.'
See you don't even have to really say anything."

And I can't do it.
I can't even repeat what he told me to say.
I just sit and look at the glowing screen
that says something about a broken teapot
and how things never work right.

FROM HERE

1. FACING EAST
I go back to the kitchen
and sit at the wooden table again,
after I put down the glass
to the tune of clouds sliding back and forth
between chimneys and airplanes
where, despite warnings of low flames,
despite missing pages,
despite uncooked disease-ridden eggs,
the splendor of moss is recognized by common women.
And then there are bowls.
The door always stays open.
Things are so bad.

2. FACING SOUTH
I come home and look at my answering machine,
the digital red zero on my answering machine,
call myself stupid and eat a frozen pizza.
It's 7:23 on a Saturday night
and I take off my bra and settle in for the evening
with the copy of *Arshile* I bought today.
In a little while the phone rings.
I jump up and answer it, "Hello."
"Can I suck all over your pussy?"
Well, I wanted someone to call
and my wish was granted.

3. Facing North

I'm going to pretend this nervous feeling
is just from the coffee but I know
that's only part of the reason.
Because even though these old wooden rafters
make everything seem light and airy
open up into outside brick room
down from my stomach broken simple and true
with strange metal things
and little copper signs like somehow
the tall door lets in and it's not me.
But it is. I get nervous thinking about
trying to use the paper cutter at Kinko's.
And I can't understand why no one's
going to be there tonight.
Brown is a comfort, though.
So dead, but it is trees and the earth,
how I call myself whole,
lie again, saying I am not utterly alone.

4. Facing West

Supposedly, we human beings are actually brighter
than the sun. We give off more light energy
per molecule or cubic inch or something.
It's just that the sun is so big.
I always wonder if I heard that right.
I mean, we're so fucking lonely.
Already I've been sitting at this yellow table for hours,
hours nobody's missing, sitting yellow, sitting here,
empty cup and a coffee-soaked napkin
and me in a chair with cowboys on the seat.
There wasn't anything for me in the paper
so I cross my fingers harder
for the resumé I sent out two weeks ago
and tell myself not to want it.
        Don't want the job.
        Don't want a new apartment.
        Don't want to write.
        Don't want more time.

Don't want something to make me stay alive
          make it easier to get up in the morning
          make flowers grow up in my eyes everywhere
          make a reason.
And all around, cars and leaves.
All around me, things are moving.
Through the leaves on the tree outside,
leaves long, thin, and pointed, swaying from side to side
sunlight lands on the floor and moves there
and on the yellow table
and even on my arm.
From millions of miles away it touches me.
I touch no one,
can't get any further than the stretch of my arms.

SPOONS

It's hot
so I have all my windows open
and so does the man
who lives in the building next door,
the big man with dark hair
whose kitchen table
is really a desk
full of papers and a briefcase.
We both take something
out of the refrigerator at the same time.
His refrigerator looks like it might be
as empty as mine usually is.
It's this living alone.
Although I did hear him
talking to someone today.
I can tell his apartment
has that same emptiness
that mine has
even with all my books and boxes.

I sit at the kitchen table for a while
then on the floor by my bed,
then on the bed.
I go to the kitchen
and get yogurt from the refrigerator.
I go back to the bed and eat it.
I throw the container away,
rinse off the spoon,
go to the bathroom,
go back to sit on the bed.
A train goes by.
I feel air from the ceiling fan.
I hear him making a clinking noise
like spoons in his apartment
just yards away.

WALKING THE RAILS TOWARD MUSIC

It may be the street, for night has fallen
over itself: has fallen into my heart and partly
has fallen has fallen hard so that day is no more
only night always falling black around me
falling and filling things up. This also means:
I have stars, tiny suns planted in my fingers.
Cracked, folded, burning, mortared, I am dark
and keep walking the rails toward music
toward angelic voices.
I walk my feet sore under the moon,
am full of sleep and dreams, use soft shallows
against my own map of rage,
but by now I have forgotten his face, forgotten warmth,
forgotten the meaning of day, of flowers,
of sitting still.

AFTER YOGA

My cats are curled up on the bed next to me,
big and bigger, sleeping.
I love my fat cat when he lies on his back
stretching out his stomach to the ceiling.
There is something so open and happy about that
that I just want to scoop him up and hug him
and rock him like a baby.
Sometimes I do.
And sometimes I stroke his belly.
Sometimes I leave him be.
It is the other one who always sits on my lap,
who curls up against me,
lies on me while I sleep.
There are days when I am amazed
at this warm living thing that comes to touch me.
If it weren't for my cats,
I could go days
without being touched by anyone.
Except me. I do touch myself.
The best is after yoga class.
I come home, take off my clothes,
and lie down on the bed,
already soft and wet before I start.
I can almost remember what it feels like to be held.
I'd have to say it's been years since I have been,
although I can't really be sure.
I have a way of erasing the past.
I like to put things behind me,
so after a certain period of time,
it can seem like things never happened at all.
And that's what it's like with this.
Although I know I've been kissed,
it's so far away that I think of myself
as someone who's never kissed anyone.
Imagine. I've never felt the tenderness
of another person's lips against mine.

KEEPING A SECRET

I am reading
The Collected Poems of Weldon Kees.
He jumped off the Golden Gate Bridge.
I also have *His Toy, His Dream, His Rest*
by John Berryman in my bag.
He jumped off a bridge too.
I work with emotionally disturbed boys
and a few weeks ago a group of them
was walking in the gully
and found a body with a gun.
The next day we know for sure
that it was someone from JPL
who had just lost his job.
Brian, my supervisor, says
what a stupid thing to do
how could anyone do that
just because he didn't have a job.
We're sitting on the stools
at the red counter
between the kitchen and the living room.
Marjorie, one of our therapists,
is standing on the other side.
I say people who kill themselves
have been feeling bad for a long time
and even though one thing
might finally trigger it,
it's something
that grows inside all your life.
Marjorie nods her head but I stop.
I see something I didn't see before—
a chasm that divides us by the fact
that I can fall in and they can't.
I stop talking,
get up and go to the dining room
where I start filling containers
of forks, spoons and napkins.

They keep talking and I keep busy
keep things filled
keep things ordered and right
and keep to myself.
I can keep a secret and I do.
No one would ever know
that I am closer to that man
in the bushes in the gully
all stiff and cold and bloody
than I am to these people
who talk and move about
as if staying alive is easy.

CUP AND SUN

No newspaper today.
It's not that I'm giving up—
I'm changing my mind,
aiming for something different.
Something shaped like sleeping eyes
and blades of grass.
Something like the equator.

If I go home, I will lie down and sleep.
And the light will slip away,
all with no peaches.
Cup and sun. Cup and sun.

At any rate, I did a good thing today—
going to the picnic
so Oscar wouldn't be the only boy
without anyone.
He ended up having a better time than Damon did;
Damon has a family
and he didn't smile until after they'd left.

Oh the clouds, oh the water, oh

the birds and signals and lines.
The sun isn't warm enough.
The arms aren't tight enough.
The poems aren't tearing my heart out enough.

The square panes of glass
distort the buildings,
curve the walls and windows,
but hardly,
not nearly
enough.

What I want to see, I won't see directly.
It's not what I want.
Not what I see when my eyes are closed.
But I will wake up again tomorrow. Oh tomorrow,
I will open my eyes anyway.

ROUND

I am drinking a cranberry ricky.
The light pink drink is in a plastic glass.
There is a white straw and about an inch of ice—
the crushed type you get in restaurants—on the top
and a slice of lime floating beneath the ice
at a 45 degree angle,
the same angle I look down on the glass,
so all I see is a thick green line straight across.
But if I turned the glass I'd see a diagonal line
or, further, the actual roundness of the lime slice.
I think about roundness.
There are different kinds—
roundness that's round all around like a ball
and roundness that sometimes doesn't look round
like the lime slice. And I am round—
not fat or well-rounded, but round somehow
just because I am more curved

than, say, straight or pointy.
But, clearly, there is a difference between
being curved and being round.
The sun is round. The moon is round and the earth.
Eyeballs are round and also the iris and pupil
that are part of the eyeball.
Oranges are round. Nipples are round.
Stoplights and rings and coins are round.
I am not round.
If, in some sudden argument at night on the street,
standing late in front of orderly houses,
beneath the street lights and stars
and some glow from some windows,
if someone's face were beginning to sweat and flush
and bits of foaming spit flew from his mouth
and in that moment of trying to make me see something,
this person pushed me to the sidewalk,
I would not roll.

MY LONG-SPENT BODY

I can't find my long-spent body.
Somewhere I left it on the way.
I tripped out of it and let go
of my headaches and teeth and moved on
to new things. Now I am like the breeze
that used to tickle my hair.
I did like my hair.
I really liked my hair.
I liked my hair and my hands,
the earring in the top of my ear
and feeling my feet hold me to the ground.

WHAT LEAVES

Let the sun-bled toes of forgiven absence
walk again toward blessings and clouded chins,

where being tiny and hollow is expected—
in fact, the only thing imaginable.

What I can do is hurt them—that is all.
And I want to deliver all those fingers,

those chewed and dirty
and the ones where warts disappear,

into some green forest
where growth is easy and everywhere

and what dies is nourishing.

I deserve the rich soil,
deserve more than my ears will allow,

but still I cry for what leaves.
I cannot hold it. I must let it go.

DIANA JEAN

diana jean was born in Toledo, Ohio, and now resides in the San Bernadino mountains with her husband, "Whale," where they conduct workshops related to the *Course in Miracles* and writing. diana jean has written many chapbooks of poetry including, *Red Tulips, I Love Toucan, Short Summer, Love Gambler* and *Terror Eyes*. Her poems have also appeared in *Spillway, Cybrocal, Verve, Red Dance Floor, Blood Pudding,* and *ONTHEBUS.*

CRYSTALS

I pick up crystal balls
every chance I get;
in dusty antique shops,
garage sales, Venice Beach, and
the metaphysical book store
on Lancaster Blvd.

Clear white glass
of different contour and sizes
arranged all along the window sill
in my kitchen.
The sun, depending on the time of day,
reflects odd rainbow shapes around.

I look into the crystal ball,
hoping to see something,
but I only see myself
upside-down reflecting back.
I never saw anyone look
into a crystal ball and know—
although I remember seeing some old movie on T.V.
about a mysterious dark-haired gypsy woman
who had on lots of jewelry.
When she looked, she knew.
I'm not sure what to look for,
although
I do look good in large earrings
and I once was mistaken
for a gypsy.

I remember the black ball filled with water
Sally brought to school. It had squares of paper
with answers written on them. You could ask
questions, like, "Does John love me?"
When you turned it upside down the answer
would appear in a little glass window at the bottom.
It never told me the answers I wanted to hear.
No boys loved me in high school.

They all wanted me to be on their baseball team.
I learned to pitch early in life.
In the war of the sexes, a girl couldn't be on
the boy's team and play the real game.
The big happening in high school
was having some boy love you and
tie angora yarn around his ring
so you could wear it.
My hands were always bigger than most of the boys'
and I knew if I ever did get a ring, it wouldn't fit.
There's no fun in that—a ring without angora,
or a black ball with pre-written messages.

Sooner or later I wanted a boy,
who in his manly body, was bigger than me.
Someone who could smile when I beat him at games.
Someone who would know that light blue angora yarn
makes me happy even if it was a sweater.

I would be able to tell him the secret of pale green
in the center of the crystals and the red and yellow too.
He wouldn't be afraid to think me magic or special.
Together we would find the answers
to my oh so many questions.

I would like to be ordinary,
like fitting in with mundane, everyday things,
instead of being seen as a witch.
But then—I'm drawn to watching the red-tail hawk
as he soars in the ravine
catching the desert thermal
just as it bumps against the mountains,
and me joining him—
dipping into the shadows,
then out into a rainbow
with just a slight rearrangement
of the very tip of my mind.

CHILDREN OR FIRE

Fire, like children,
never belongs to anyone.
Individual at conception,
growth dependent
only with the direction
of the wind
the spaces between
the trees
and the incline
of the mountains
encountered
along the way.

BLACK CAT, BLUE SNAKE

I pulled the blue strip off the
gallon bottle of low-fat milk.
It lies on a square
of tile in the kitchen.
Coiled, icy blue and waiting.
Milk-top viper in the
twinkle of a cat's perspective.
The cat crouches low and sleek,
shorter than ears.
His belly sucks
the floor in a
snail's pace.
No distance from paw to shoulder.
No eyelash or whisker flinches
as the cat stalks
its snake in slow motion.
Eclipsed cat—so
deadly quiet and poised.
Mostly he is being invisible

so he can get it.
He sits so still.
You know that in the stillness
of the moment, something
is going to happen.
He leaps,
leaps and snatches the blue snake
with just the curve of a well-placed claw,
tosses it into the air.
The snake mimicks the cat's body,
leaps into the air itself.
Free of earthly thoughts,
just for an instant,
cat and snake celebrate
the absence of gravity.
Together they return to
the smooth surface of the Indian tile
to slide and glide in different directions,
until nothing moves.
The whole thing starts again;
the prey unaware of the cat,
of the cat's yellow eyes
and sharp claws,
white-fanged hunter
gone wild.

IN THE FIELDS

The nail shop in Palmdale is owned
by Vietnamese, husband and wife.
He does the design and she fills in behind.
They have three children and cook rice
in the back room for lunch. They still have
relatives and friends in Vietnam.
He used to be a captain in the Vietnamese Navy.
His hands are smaller than mine. Hand to hand
combat would be a fair fight. No arguments

as I pick Moonlight for my nail polish.
It matches my dress, otherwise
no one would pick it, white is so Sixty-ish.
Bob liked my nails the color of moonlight.
He liked the back seat
of his fifty-five Chevy.
I wore a remembrance bracelet
when he left for Vietnam.
He never came back.
He died a hero on some hill
I couldn't find on the map.
I didn't go to the funeral either.
When I went to Washington D.C. six years ago,
I looked for his name on the black wall.
I only had a scrap of paper
and I borrowed a green pencil from a woman,
who was looking for her son's name.
I found Bob's name easily,
not too high or too low,
just there, near the beginning.
I put the paper on his name and
rubbed the pencil over it.
I looked for the piece of paper when I moved.
It was lost,
but I found the bracelet and a snapshot.
Bob is standing in front of his blue and white car,
his hand shading his eyes from the summer sun.
There is an alfalfa field in the background and
a decadent grin on his face.
The kind that meant our roaming of Lancaster backroads
had paid off. An alfalfa field with no harvesters
or rain-birds—it was perfect to put the red blanket on.
Cool sweet-smelling grass,
the alfalfa so high it made four walls of thick green.
Bob kissed my white pearl fingertips,
as if each was his favorite,
I laid my head back on the blanket,
like you do in the field.
Love was innocent on that summer day.
I was just fifteen; Mama never suspected.

LOVE TAKES PARTS OF YOU

I can't seem to trust
the permanence of the day.
Everything is the same, yet
everything is different.
Me, especially,
my courage buried with that dog.
I can't get back on track, can't remember what it was
I was doing, or
if there was something particular
that I needed to start, but there doesn't seem to be a finish line,
or a starting line, for that matter.

No one seems to know about this,
how I feel or
even that my dog died.
But it is more than that, you know,
it's the giving up of parts of myself.
Out of control, and I hate it.
Now I want to hold tight to all of me
who I was or at least think I am,
I am no longer sure,
if I ever had a real grip.
If I ever cast a true shadow, because
I have learned to travel
camouflaged in the trees
leaving no footprints in the leaves.

I mean if I died this minute
I'm not so sure there would be anyone
to cry over me like I been crying over
that old white dog.
There'd be nobody
to be placed in the ground.
No need for flowers or sentimentality.
No one left behind
who isn't whole.

STONE DOG

This is a poem about a spiritual dog,
Who is running for all the dogs
That cannot run, because
They do not have a mountain to run on.

He streaks across the mountain top
The wind in his eyes.
Earth below passes swiftly by
Blurring sounds of earth and sky
Leaving only the thump of galloping paws
Digging up the dirt to fly.

Walking never a consideration now—
Winged, he runs
Not touching one blade of grass on the ground
Or stumbling to the earth,
A dog speeding, not aware of any
Other time,
Just now.

"I prefer transport on the sparrow's foot,"
Says rock. "I'm mystifying."
Check out the clouds rolling over
Salty tango dips and rocking stones,
As she looks at the dancing pebble
That was herself.

Dog has four legs under him
And remembers that the trail
Is like a dream. He said: "See here,
I speed through the cold of
Winter, and Summer warms
My flag-waving tail."
He keeps coming back
To run the mountain.

He runs the quickest path,
His white ears flatten.
The wind whispers
Of a past secret moment.
He died before.
The trees were never so green as now.
The path so easily taken
Far from everyone.

BLUE, EGO BENCH MARK

This is the first day
of the second half of the year.
The time has rushed by since Xmas
and the snow, cold, scary time
of not knowing about my future.
Worse, not caring.
If I could have disappeared,
vanished without violence or pain,
I would be gone now.

I would not be here to see
winter end or spring come.
Not know about the snow in March,
or a new thrush's nest of baby birds.
Not hear the scream of the locust
that only happens every seven years.

But here I am with a warm breeze
blowing through the kitchen window.
Guess I'm happy.
Yes, happy.
So happy my ears could almost blow off.

"I'm happy," I think I'd better whisper it
in a small voice,
for fear someone will overhear,

some shadow person
will snatch up my peace and joy.
Covet it as some culprit,
stealing it away and
then it will be gone—
Gone.

I never worried when
I was lonely and scared,
not even friends remembered
my phone number,
or came down a two-mile dirt road
to see me,
let alone some ominous
sneaky theft in the night.
Someone standing around waiting to
capture all the blue time.
Holding it for ransom,
or just keeping it.
No one fears that.
I don't think so anyway.

But, now the blue is in the sky.
Joy is in my heart,
happiness fills me,
but I'm vigilant
and look behind me
from time to time,
just in case.

ALL FOR A SONG

From the first woman and first man,
the first pen, the first A,
undeniable is our artist thrust to create.
"I have a hard time," he said,
"with the idea of poetry;

we should understand hearing it:
I must hear it sing."
Poetry demands all.
It eviscerates Stellasue, Elizabeth Bishop,
Jack Grapes—these followers of the Muse:
courageous elaborators of process.
Grapes said Lowell gouged the air
and remembered not the past owl.
Struggling poets cannot survive.
No one to protect them from the critic's evil eye,
protest of man the poets' own words
levied against their creative spirits:
The only words that are not their demise
are the words written from their hearts—
that set them free.

SLEEPLESS NIGHT WITH STORM

The clouds pack together,
leaving no space for thunder to burp
or blue to show.

Nature has the right.
The water drops from the sky
raging down freeways,
rolling mobile homes
over on their sides.
A cat giving up to the energy,
sleeps in the afternoon,
its slotted eyes show green,
yellow, aqua iridescence
that glows in the dark,
secrets of the night are known.
The wind takes
the silver of the moon
from behind the clouds.
The oceans turns

and flips me onto the rocks.

In the dream
my eyes float from behind my hands.
When I'm hiding,
I don't want to look.
When I do look I still don't see.
I shut my eyes tight
to see the quiet
inside my own lids.

What comfort there is is in the darkness:
when my feet find the path
of frozen wood and edges,
when the wood laid at diagonals
in Indian patterns
steps flat to a downhill line,
when I follow my heartbeat home.

DREAMS

A thought
A second
A lifetime
Of imagining
Myself different
Than I am
Until I become
That which I dream

MIFANWY KAISER

Mifanwy Kaiser teaches writing arts in Southern California. Her work appears in journals such as *Voices, On Target, Spillway, ONTHEBUS,* and in the anthology *News From Inside.* She currently edits *Spillway.*

SIMPLE GIFTS

I am in Washington.
I've come to Schooner's Beach,
and created a nest for a week.
On a bench seat by the window
in the living room
I watch the ocean, the trees, the birds.

I like this house. It's not chopped up
into boxes except for two bedrooms
and a bathroom along one wall.
The living, dining, and kitchen areas
flow into each other.

Early this morning I put bread out
on the porch railings.
Two crows circled for quite some time
then landed, cawing on the roof.
They flew to the each of the four corners
of the property,
landed in each area of the pine trees
that protect this house,
then flew to the railing to feed.

I found two feathers this afternoon . . .
long black ones on the porch
where they had been feeding . . .
simple gifts.

Last night the sky turned blue black.
The trees across the cove
darkened into silhouettes.
I watched them lean against the wind,
slanting just slightly—
not fighting against it—
but flowing with it.
The ocean waves rolled up against the shore.

Two days ago I jogged on the beach at 6:30 a.m.

I am alone. It's misting.
I run from one end to the other,
tap my right foot on the rocks at each end.

Coming back I find a sand dollar.
I've looked for one since I was ten
when I saw a picture in a library book.
Finally, at 46 I find one right in front of me.

So this is how it's done.
I find treasures in my life by stumbling
onto things right in front of me.

BUTTERFLY WINGS

The seamstress did fold that curb last road past.
Her fingers winked at me asked politely then
ginger-jerked back for her falling body so
almost crunched up tight winking needles at me
making tumbles candling back over young boy wick.

So I come to know the limits
of me, of that part of me
that doesn't speak
doesn't imagine
doesn't love
doesn't feel
the tread that holds me.

I close my eyes then open them.
I turn my key in the lock very slowly.
Dark caverns open like giant mouths or eyes
sticking their tongues out over moss.
The wind blows smoothe over dry and cracked skin, kissing
it moving body hairs like leaves of trees.

My nipples move.

I rub my hand over each one, feel their ridges.
They are petaled like the blooms of chrysanthemums
moving to the furry back of the butterfly just landed there
waiting to be stroked.

Blossoms strain out to my mouth
tongue stick out wet, moist
reaches mums wanting
wanting watering
wanting licking
wanting sucking
hand strokes fire, tongue licks
hand strokes fire, tongue licks
hand strokes fire, tongue licks
hand strokes fire wings together
beats flutters beats flutters
beats flutters together alone
alone together alone together
alone together alone together
alone to alone to alone alone alone
alone.

The red pepper is blooming again.
It's taken a long time but it's
finally blooming again alone.

ON THE EDGE

It's in the morning that I notice
on my drive to school
just as I turn the corner
the trees lined up straight, erect.

They have no blooms in the morning.
They're naked, stripped bare and barren
just on the edge of the concrete.
A white cloud blue of the sky grasps them
the branches open and wide, waiting

waiting for me.

It happens every year at the same time,
in the second week of April.
On my way home in the afternoon,
I look up and these same trees,
almost unnoticed, are in full bloom,
flowered in white and green
opening to some silence, some finger
that grows and creeps up from the earth
and touches the roots of these beauties,
their branches splayed open
waiting for me
waiting for my silent finger
to prod them into bloom.

DUSTING

God is a woman you know.
I saw her last night in the fire
just before she stepped out of it
to pull the blanket up around my chin.

I know it was her.
She said my name three times
just before she drew me in.

Once before she stood by my bed,
once when she held out her hand,
and one time just before her secrets took me.

I know they took me because
lately, I've been tending the garden—
putting lilies, sweetpeas, roses on the hearth;
watching the sky more closely;
keeping lighted candles in the hall.
I've been feeding the visiting birds
and playing with the cats that stroll through the yard

on their way to whatever it is that cats do.

Lately, just lately
I've been dusting.

OBSESSION

It flings boulders
out of dark caves crouching
at the back of churchyards

The crunching thudding
of the flung
the rounding sounds the set jaw
Christ! the set jaw jowls hurt
when you practice piano playing
the notes away
to no one who hears
who wants to hear anyways
it's not here then yet

hear hear heard have heard

ah, but the herding of the mouth
toward the sex of it
throbbing inside
watching another mouth
churn, sling, poke
slurring tongue-taste toward
the coming of it
half-gag
swallow.

PEELING POTATOES

She sits at the kitchen table
peeling potatoes,

scraping
the skin from them
gouging
the eyes out
with soft and gentle hands.

After she has scraped and gouged,
she quarters them and puts them
into the water, boiling, breathing, panting,
in the pot beside her.

After the last has been scraped
and gouged and quartered,
after she puts the knife down,
after she gets up,
walks to the stove,
stands there with her back to me,
wipes her hands on her apron,

I slip into someone else
pick up the knife, clench my fingers
around the handle, get up, go to her
stand behind her, reach around her
and give my mother this knife.

MOURNING ROOM

Sometimes I don't cry at funerals.
I've seen the same thing happen several times to others.
They let their eyes wander around the mourning room,
get up and file past the casket
with the other people gathered there,
perhaps focus on a particular bouquet
or person in the room, and then at the grave
send some of themselves into the earth.

HUMMING AGAIN

The fan in the kitchen is humming again,
a constant low-pitched sound
at the churning of the blades against
the air at the top of the room
just below the crawl space in the attic.
It's not really an attic.
It's the space between the ceiling and the roof—
dead space.
Nothing's up there except beams,
insulation, and termite droppings—
droppings from where they found our house
and settled in to bore away a life for themselves.

COMING TO KNOW

I remember the prison in Kentucky
Just down the street
from the high school where I also taught.
Actually the street is a road.
In winter the trees along it
are frosted with ice and if the sun
catches them just right
they look like delicate crystal
arms and fingers reaching
up and out.

Not many escapes happen in winter.
The men know they can't run
fast enough over ice and snow.
They stand at the windows,
reach up and out,
but stay where they are.

They are good students for me.
They set and break the state record

for the number of GEDs issued
through the prison system.
Ours is one of the smallest populations.
When they pass their test
their names are engraved in bronze and added
to the plaque outside the classroom door.
They bring their wives, lovers, children
mothers, fathers
to see their names.

What is in their prison files doesn't fit
these people I come to know.
On file they are people who have done
terrible, terrible things.
They have raped.
They have murdered.
They have abused their children.

A word like rape isn't alive until
you read transcripts of the trial proceedings
details of what is done
the small tiny details

I heard the door slide open
I thought I was dreaming then
I felt someone
in my room
oh god, I tried to scream
tried to move but couldn't
He leapt on top of me growling
grunting jerked my arms
behind me and tied my wrists
I begged him not to hurt me as he
pushed my face into the pillow
and spread my buttocks
and rammed his penis into
my anus then
he shoved me over and pried
my teeth open with hands
in leather gloves and stuck

his penis down my throat up and down, up and down,
I could smell and taste my feces I choked
and vomited
it gushed out of my throat and nostrils
down the sides of my mouth
he grabbed my inner thich and squeezed
my legs open and grunted
into my vagina
then he untied me, said "Thanks cunt," and left
through my front door
afterwards I could hear him breathing
I tried to call the operator
but I couldn't remember the number

and then
you come to know the word without experiencing it.

and why women are afraid of it.

It's those tiny details going on forever.

I'm afraid of it.

and sometimes when I'm alone and sleeping
with the patio door open in summer
I hear noises that aren't there or I'm hoping
aren't there and I get a tightness in my chest
and I have to get up to turn the lights on
and I get this strange thought that I'm not as
afraid of being murdered as I am of being raped
and I'd like to believe it's because my chances of
being murdered are far less than being raped.

But if I'm really honest, it's that I don't want
to be that vulnerable . . . ever
I don't want to be that aware
I'm vulnerable
to have to live with those details
I only know from reading.

Life is supposed to be delicate.

And I try to understand how a man
can be so kind, so helpful
so delicate
like crystal arms and fingers
he won't be up for parole for years
so gentle in the prison school
then turn so violent, so hideous
on paper.

MOTHER TALK

The kitchen smells of ammonia.
My mother gives me my first permanent.
I'm twelve at the kitchen table
my mother behind me
my sister in front—
she's fifteen.

In between wrapping and twisting
my hair, my mother talks about
school, boys, dating and my birth.

I'm a difficult baby to carry—
restless and kicking
waves of nausea
morning after morning into morning.
I'm more difficult to deliver
stubborn
mum says I wouldn't budge for
thirty-six hours.

Not like my sister—she's easy—
slips out in grace.
But I cramp, jab, hack
my way here
surprise her

I'm tiny
like a sparrow she says
and Dad
and then back to pain and blood
as she saturates my hair
with perm solution.

Just as the last curl is saturated,
the last curl at the back of my neck,
just when I pull the towel
away from my face
I faint into my sister's lap
and then into thirty
when I give myself my last permanent
before I drive myself to the hospital
check myself in
then drive myself home
after I've had myself sterilized.

A CERTAIN LIGHT

There's a certain sky that comes
after a night rain that's
blue and black and white
and the gulls that fly there
turn themselves to the sun just
coming out and shine like angel's wings.

STELLASUE LEE

STELLASUE LEE'S work is published in two books: a collection of four Los Angeles poets, *After I Fall*, and an exchange of poems with David Widup, *Over To You* (Bombshelter Press). She is also poetry editor for Rattle, a literary magazine. In 1991, she was given an award by the Board of Library Commisioners and Mayor Tom Bradley for storytelling in the Los Angeles public libraries. She received her Ph.D from Honolulu University. Her work has been widely published. She was born in the year of the dragon.

THE QUEEN OF JACKS

Jacks was my game.
Early morning
sitting on cold concrete
picking up splits
with the sweep of my hand.
I knew where to toss the ball,
and just how high.
I was the Queen of Jacks.
The boys would be around the corner
pitching pennies,
or shooting marbles
(all in the thumbs),
bragging over some old cat's eye
or puree;
boulders were the big ones.
But I was the Queen of Jacks,
a title that never followed me anywhere.
Just a string-bean kid with limp colorless hair,
telling Mother she was supposed to be home
when I got there with a glass of milk,
and two, that's two cookies.
I wore an anklet with my name engraved on it
just to identify myself.
Nine years old,
and taking my lunch money across the street
to the soda fountain; climbing up on a swivel stool
and asking for "The Usual,"
which meant apple pie a la mode.
I can tell you,
there were plenty of days
I gagged on that good thing,
but it could've been liver
and I would have eaten it,
just so the next day I could walk in and say,
"The Usual,"
and the guy behind the counter knew
the Queen of Jacks was there for lunch.

CROWS

Crows are usually plentiful along my street
dropping nuts from up high
then swooping down to sort through the remains
but on this day
for no good reason I can think of
I was watching from the window
and thinking how strange
that not one of these large black birds
was anywhere in sight
when a woman
leading the teeniest dog on a red leash
whose long shaggy fur gave the illusion
of a mop skittering along the street
must have felt a tug
as one of these crows
swooped down out of the sky
and snatched the dog and leash
right out of the woman's clutches
leaving us both open mouthed
and staring up at the early morning sky
and the last I saw of either the crow
or the dog
was one final glimpse
as they were flying directly into a rising sun
coming up out of the canyon
past trees and the hilly countryside
just beyond the great city of Los Angeles

MONTEREY

It has stopped raining.
That's a start at any rate,
even in bed I'm cold.
I know what they mean when they say "cold to the bone."
The bone in my foot aches; the one I broke years ago.
Even in a knee-chest position,

even with my heavy winter coat over the covers,
I am cold to the bone.

And this house, this house is so saturated it droops;
the windows are swollen,
the doors must be forced open and closed.

I put on the warmest clothes I can find,
a heavy Polo sweat shirt with a hood.
Its cheerful red seems out of place.
Hoping for some comfort,
I take the winding path down to the sea.
The wind is punishing.

Gulls fly circles overhead.
A pelican dives headfirst into the water.
No muss, no fuss. A clean, easy kill.

A lone fisherman appears,
and sets up his gear on the sand.
He smiles. I smile.
It's a reflex action.

Back at the house, I think,
my friend should be waking up.
It will be her first day home from the hospital.
It's near the end, they say.
Near the end.

NO WAY HAS YET BEEN INVENTED TO SAY GOODBYE

I'd flown, Burbank/Las Vegas: Las Vegas/Burbank.
It was late, and I was tired.
Rather than join the rush to exit,
I stay in my seat and watch the ground crew

clear out the underbelly of the plane.
I don't have any luggage,

just a new book of poems by Jim Harrison;
the one dedicated to his brother's child;

dead at fifteen. Gloria . . . Gloria.
I watch a canvas bag
with a big red heart sewn on its side
bump along,
throbbing it seems.

Finally the stewardess comes for me
has to remind me it's time to leave;
time for the cleaning crew to come aboard.
The captain and co-pilot follow me down the ramp.

I turn the corridor in time to see the two men link arms
and whistling different tunes, shuffle sideways.
Somewhere, someone claps.
I am quick to weep.

The days have been back-to-back clouds,
my spirit broken as easily as a wishbone.
Gloria . . . Gloria . . . Gloria.
I used to have a gun in the house.

It wasn't the cold, black of the thing that frightened me.
It was me, fear of what I might do.
I held its coldness to my forehead once,
hoping to freeze the fire inside.

I think she must have drowned. Jim never says,
but much of the book is about water.
Last night I had this dream: I was swimming
at the bottom of the sea, so alone, it's deadly.

LISTEN, PLEASE LISTEN

I lie down for a nap, but every time I close my eyes
whitecaps heave the bed around.

I've forgotten the feeling of safety
in his arms.

The night is quiet,
a sleeping volcano.

The phone rings twice,
then nothing.

Lately, I've been looking
in a magnifying glass.

Listen, please listen.

The sky flashes electric,
SEX SEX SEX SEX . . .

My hands are numb,
and I have grit in my teeth.

I'm building walls again.
We haven't made love in months.

Left lane, left ventricular, left hand,
left brain, nothing is right tonight.

It's Tuesday,
he just turns on the television.

Now I cry
only on odd numbered days.

I can't imagine Christmas coming.

BURYING THE PILLS

For Albert J. Chacon: October 16, 1962 - May 24, 1995

May 24:
the tree outside my second-story window
is in full dress now,
except for the brown leaves
of the broad leaf ivy,
left clinging to the trunk
after being severed at the ground.
It climbed higher than a smart cat would climb.

Yesterday I saw a squirrel in the tree.
Today, a hummingbird flies in place
looking over the dead vine.
The bird's iridescent blue body
gathers the morning spring sun,
or what there is of it.

Once, when I was only five,
our neighbor's house was broken into.
The woman who lived there
was pregnant, and expecting twins.
So that she would remember to take her morning pills,
she lined them up on the kitchen windowsill.
It was unusually warm for spring,
and that window had been left ajar.
This is how the thief entered,
first placing the pill bottles on the ground.

It doesn't matter what was taken.
What I remember was finding those pills
early the next morning
before anyone was even aware
that a burglary had taken place,
and having been told the pills grew babies,
I planted them between the two ribbons of concrete
that led to the garage in back.

Tomorrow I'll walk with my head bent
toward the ground
with dirt clenched in each fist.
Ashes to ashes, dust to dust
I'll chant the Rosary in the shower.
I'll tear the collar of my dress.
I'll wander through the surf
and listen to the murmur of each wave.

Lord, grief has weighed me down so
that I'm sinking in losses:
Mother, Father, all the babies

still nestled in their little dirt beds;
and friends, so many friends
have stepped out of their bodies,
gone waving their arms into the night.

SPILT MILK

I've heard it all my life—
someone's mother is always saying
"No sense crying over spilt milk,"
but after two cups of my special blend
of coffee and milk,
and while making the third,
the last of the milk misses the cup
and spreads across the kitchen counter
in a white wash.

I can't stop crying.
Sobs fill the room.
How long has such grief been traveling?
How is it that I woke at 5,
showered, made the bed
and fed the cats
just like it was any other morning?

Grief drives the cats under the bed.
In time, I too work my arm and one shoulder
under the bed into their dusky cave
with its heavy, unblinking stillness.

I wish to be small-small as a cat;
to curl under the bed,
blue carpeting my cushion;
the underside of the mattress,
my white sky.

Anyone who stopped here would frown.

I wouldn't blame them;
a small alabaster body in a cave;
kitchen tiles glazed white,
and grief—such grief,
free to roam from room to room
waiting to be fed.

REPORT

I read it in the newspaper:
a woman, naked,
covered in blood,
was seen walking
the old Townsgate section
of Westlake.
The police were called,
but when they arrived
she had disappeared.
I tell you this now:
It was me; stripped bare, bloodied,
I walked from my marriage.
That was last winter.
My footprints were quickly shrouded
by the brightly colored leaves
of orange and gold.
This is California after all;
a sun without ending
devours the years.

A mouse languishes in a rat trap.
The roof springs a leak.
Dust gathers along the floorboards.
Now the killing season of acceptance
is on me, L.A. shakes my nerves
as I drive its rioting streets.

FEBRUARY'S FLOWERS

To see just how far I'd come,
I took the pillow from the other side of the bed
and put it behind my back.
This was my husband's pillow,
the one that cradled his head.
I'd thought about cushioning my back
from the hard wood of the headboard before,
but hadn't wanted to claim
that side of the bed.
I'm careful at night too,
never to stray from my own flowered side.
Now my feet—
that's a different story—
it seems they have a mind of their own,
so used to resting against his warm calf.
They search, wake me with their cold findings.

Winter

has come.
I fling a heavy quilt over the bed.
Now when I slide between the flowered sheets, my head drunk with fatigue,
I sleep—sleep and dream:
Roses bursting forth with dazzling fragrance;
pink azaleas with ten thousand separate blooms;
green blades of grass trembling toward the sun,
and yellow buttercups dusting the air;
the earth radiant, and me,
surprised to find myself still alive.

CIRCLES

Bob says Stellasue and I say Bob,
and he says, I like that piece you read tonight.
I say, thanks guy but truth is,

all this writing about my childhood
has started me thinking, and I'm reminded
of when I was teaching tennis in Europe.
I say, I played the European Tennis Circuit in '70,
and every chance I got
I'd go to an American army base
and offer tennis lessons
to pick up a few extra dollars.
One day it dawned on me
that some people are afraid of getting hit by the ball.
I see that Bob understands,
so I tell him that I'd make a point of hitting them.
I say, I'd pick a place on their arm or thigh,
and hit them with the ball.
Bob looks stunned to think I'd do such a thing,
and I tell him, they were horrified at having been hit,
but I'd run over and ask if they were hurt.
Then I'd tell them to draw a circle around the spot
that had been hit.
By this time the shock has worn off,
and feeling a bit foolish,
they'd draw a circle.
On a scale of one to ten, ten being worst, I'd ask,
how much does it hurt?
I'd tell them the reason they were having difficulty
returning more than two or three balls
is their fear of getting hit.
Bob, I say,
I think that's what Jack is having me do by writing all this stuff,
'cause I have to tell ya, I'm running out of abusive situations
to write about, and I feel like I've drawn a few circles;
I'm surprised too, I say,
I haven't been hurt as bad as I thought.
Bob stands there comfortable in his big frame,
nodding and looking wise,
and when he speaks, his voice is so quiet,
I have to strain to hear him.
Ah yes, he says, we all have circles to draw.

TELL ME AGAIN

for Robert Thais

About the time you and one of your girls
drove by that place in Northridge
that sells cords of firewood,
and she said, "Daddy look,
somebody chopped up their whole house."
Tell me that one again.

And the one about that Sunday morning,
how you were reading in bed and your daughter
curled up beside you,
patted the day-old growth on your face,
and said, "Poor Daddy has little tiny splinters
all over his face."
That was a good one.

And that time she asked you for money,
and you gave her a dime, how she handed it back
and said, "No Daddy, give me some green stuff."
That one never fails to make me smile.

Tell me about the time your oldest girl
was crying because she wanted something
her younger sister had;
how she put her head in your lap
while the younger one stood in the doorway
sucking her thumb, watching.
And when you comforted the one crying child,
the younger one came over and stroked her sister's leg;
told her, "Life isn't always easy."
Tell me that one again.

PRISCILLA LEPERA

PRISCILLA LEPERA lives in the San Fernando Valley with her husband and young daughter. She graduated from the University of Massachusetts at Amherst with a degree in English.Priscilla   was a co-editor and co-founder of *Tsunami*, a small poetry magazine, from 1987 to 1989.

THE PIZZAMAN AT COSTCO

I love him, I tell Betty.
Yeah, he's great, she says.
No, I say, *I love him*
and I jab the cart with my hand
while the kids twitter at our feet.
Once, Hayley's foot got stuck
but that was another day.
Today, I order pizza
in my best, my sweetest
voice.

The pizzaman, I worry about
him. His face is foursquare,
his cheeks shoot straight
into temples, Palladian,
you could say, or homely,
the way light recurs
along his scalp in waves
of grey. How familiar he seems,
though we've never met
except to hand him my
three dollars and twenty-five cents.
Thank you O thank you!
But he never sees, not even
to tender. He just takes the
money and looks precisely
past me while his hands
braille the keys. This never
focusing is queer. Betty,
I say, what is a fortysomething
pizzaman with cleanshaven nails
and a military air doing here?
But it's for me to worry:
what ships he leaves uncaptained,
what crises unaverted,
what debates peglegged
by his absence.
The world is missing him.

Pizzaman,
however you end up here
in Van Nuys, just off Sepulveda,
shoving slices of pizza into cardboard
triangles for hungry matrons like me,
whatever brought you to this
fucky world of yearning
and mere decency,
I love loss best in you,
as in myself.

When you step to your mirror tonight,
whatever hands betray you,
whatever last chance malingers
at your bedstead,
do look
let yourself look straight on
without flinching
let your silver
mysterious
hair down
entirely.

MESSAGE UNRECEIVED

My daughter sleeps all crazy
slamming her arms and legs
into the mattress, all the while
drooling and grinding her teeth
until I tap her cheeks to stop.
I can feel her jaw bones grinding.
Her molars crunch and gnash,
as she tosses herself around.
Sometimes, she falls right out.
The body thumps to the floor—
I come running from somewhere else
to find her limp with sleep.
She doesn't wake
when I lift her

to the very middle of the bed,
but clicks and works her teeth,
and turns her face into the pillow.
I go back to whatever it was
I was doing, wondering why
she never bruises herself,
what she's dreaming
that sets her teeth to Morse code.
But I have the gift of sorrow
and I think I know:

her teeth are too angry to lie still,

her bones are soft
and seek the place
they can never leave.
They would like to lie
with finality, undisturbed.
They know they can last
forever.

But the flesh is afraid to stop.
Dreaming or real, it's all her life,
which the flesh moves through
and loves and can't let go.
Sun, moon, rain, dinner, crayons—
the flesh sees how it is—
this short, crummy life
is all you get.
Already, the flesh rebels.

Though noisy, the teeth
really have nothing to signify,
save this grinding of pearls
to phosphorescence.
Luminous-tongued,
my twitching daughter
suffers the long night
in her carnal grotto,
dreaming of oysters

and all things
nacreous.

EXALTATION

*"Over every blade of grass
there stands an angel saying Grow"*
Talmud

"The Angel of Alphabets opens the door..."
Nancy Willard

Oh, nothing of dungeon and dread.
No threat of malebolge, no adamantine chains
or brittle-winged harpy, braying of sins
and stuck on our disobedience.
No false cathedral voice, stone-lipped,
to drone demerit in Latinate clause;
No magnificent blinding of kin, no coddle of kine
or pale cast of unreal sanctimony—
no splendor too dear for human eyes—
those lead-fallen gods who rise with flood
to claim the earth cold-spun of stone and dumb,
forsake us for ether.

No, none of these,
but something like a cupid,
rosy and mortal-seeming
plush of wingbud and lip,
round-bellied, dimpled, smallish, useful.
Gravitate hither, tiny host,
gladden my family
and glorify my rooms.
Say, the angel of coffee,
sweetly abrew in the a.m.,
one perfect cup floats to me before I ask
on a whisper of wings.
Then, the angel of French toast
and occasionally, marmelade.
Beloved of children and old ladies,
she arrives with a sticky kiss.
The grim angel of laundry never smiles

but that's o.k.—she has stern work to do,
stigmata to remove. I leave her to suds.
The gentle angel of dust motes arrives mid-morning,
gilding the air simply with her presence.
I remember her from my crib days
(she whom my mother chased with a flannel)
only to find her, years later,
crackling over the intercom,
static that falls on the sleeping baby's face —
O, kindness of dust!
History of dust!
Best and oldest angel,
falling (not fallen) and onto every sill, of every room,.
a pure, refractor of light. . .

So what if it's just my dirty kitchen,
some tepid coffee, yesterday's breakfast,
and everywhere, clutter, cobwebs, dirt?
That most mornings start with a fight,
a drawer slammed, me cursing and tripping over things
and everyone in tears?
The thing is,
something pushes me out the door every morning,
wiping crumbs from the corners of my mouth
and folding back the edges of my sleeves
to keep them clean.

You could call it angels
or anything that says: This is the world!
Get up!

So I do—
I go outside and there are the brown hills
at the end of the street, sturdy as ever.
And here is my neighbor, Dave the plumber,
going off to unclog things.
And across the way, my other neighbor, Jess,
rips up tar to make a new driveway.
"Looking good," I yell.

And Susan and Michael get into their truck
with their three children,
the youngest of whom is wailing,
but the door slamming muffles it.
They're my favorite family,
so I wave a lot and promise myself
to visit them later.
Then Hayley and I quit bickering
so she can go to kindergarten.
She climbs into the car humming a little tune
she has just made up. (She'll sing it all day,
until I catch her eye in the rearview mirror.
Then she'll stick out her tongue
and look away, annoyed. I know what
she means, how it's good to be alone
with your song, sometimes.)
Then Bruce comes out scowling
but unwilling to send us off without a goodbye
or some sign that we lead reasonable lives.
I start to scowl back
but the dialectic of sunny and all demands grace,
so I crank down the window
and try to be nice, grudgingly at first,
until I find that my whole self
wants to be happy,
this fine morning.
When he leans in the window,
I rub a kiss along his beard
and think what an asshole I am,
how I don't deserve this little family,
this home, these puny comforts.
All right, my life's not perfect—
sometimes it downright stinks—
Yet, here is the grass so greenly up
that a swallowtail
just now arisen
on buttery wings,
transfigures lawn,
and street and all of us
in her wake.

I know I overstate things but thank you,
O angel of lucky-to-be-here,
of (count them) your blessings—
all you angels of ordinary joy.

AUBADE

My daughter's a disappointment
There—I've said it.
She hates to read, she tells me.
I go crazy, of course—
I don't want an ignoramous around the house
so I throw a bowl of Cheerios on the table,
and stomp away.
I don't care, I yell,
and slam my bedroom door.
Then I lock it for good measure.
M-M-Mommy, she whispers, when I come out,
Aren't you gonna take me to school?
No, I say, without looking, Daddy can do it.
So she bends in for a hug,
with her big, serious eyes,
but I won't.
I just push her away.
She looks like she would like to cry
but I hand her the umbrella, turn my back.
Get going, I yell over my shoulder.
I go to the shower and slam the door,
half thrilled to be slamming
and half afraid the cheesy glass will shatter.

Then I'm under the water
thinking terrible thoughts.
I clench my teeth
I think about hitting her,
hitting anyone.
I swing my bare arms,
splashing hot water on the tiles
and the fogged-up glass.

I can't see—
there's nothing to see—
just air and water—
but it's enough to send me,
dripping and wrapped in my towel,
running to the front door,
which I yank open.
Goodbye, Goodbye, I yell to their profiles
on the other side of the windshield.
On the front seat of the pickup,
they face each other—
I can see them—
Hayley's perfect nose,
Bruce, nodding his beard—
I know what he's telling her.
I watch them go
as I would some great natural disaster,
some ax or infant's slow descent
just beyond my fingers.
I try to stop it
but fall they must,
for I am a wielder of axes,
tipper of cradles,
a breaker of boughs.

Goodbye, GOODBYE, I yell again
but they swing out from the driveway
and never see me.

It's 8:53 a.m., February 8, 1995.
Let the day begin.
I know what I've done.

ALWAYS THE DOVES

With round, low note—
mourning or not, I couldn't say—
but more like a foghorn—
it's a very grey day.

Then a bicycle wings by—
the sidewalk heaves slightly in its wake
and still no tricks, no shield, no beam-me-up.
His slouchbag contains exactly silver.
This is not the age of Rapid Transit.

My mother has that immaculate conception.
I mean, the macular degeneration
of her eyes, which have it.
My own are brown or, rather,
the off-green of decay,
all mossy fern and duckweed,
entropic, pond-slime green.
Dull bracken rims the cornea,
and at center, there's leafmeal
(the brown of my driver's license).
Well, I would wish for seafoam candy green,
more nearly blue, or bluish,
a touch of orpiment and aqua.
But I walk through fur and entrails,
the world of my dark eye complete
and bevelled like the horizon,
ideal, as in a painting, or even posterity,
which is rarely seen.

When I cannot see, am stopped—
when I stop—
for nothing's there—
will it be there?
My eyes, before coin of close,
will they cloud or clear or darken, untearing
or gaze through hook of grieving flesh (will grieve?)
to fix on ferry and Asphodel?

Then I'll say, Hermes, get me,
I'm ready as rain
but you must lead
for my eyes become marbles
and my feet are but wood.
And I look up from writing this—

how nothing's changed!—
all bold and placid blooms,
all awful, looming sky—Oh, how will it manage without me?
Still to go to The Pancake House?
And stand in line with a paper,
worrying about investments
and boring, teenage sons,
eating German pancakes, which I love. . .
Who'll order when I'm gone?
And how shall they exist?

And how dare you, I call from my bier of smoke,
How dare you go on!
Then, stiff and ponderous, no longer toothsome,
I set them to keen, castrato-like, over me,
wailing to fade as my coronet fades
on a lampshade in my mother's faraway house,
a dusty, nuptial folly,
hardly even a souvenir.
Go into the land, I would tell myself then,
go into it.
But already,
I'm there.

OLD NOW

Look, I said, look, we're old now, we're old.
We live alone. Our set's on the blink.
I go where I go with nothing to hold.

Did you imagine it would be so cold?
I never thought I'd have to think.
Look, I said, look, we're old now, we're old

and I went through the hall and began to unfold
some dust that I keep in a drawer by the sink.
I go where I go with nothing to hold.
There may be an answer to something foretold

in a dull life lived hard on the brink.
Look, I said, look, we're old now, we're old

My children exist to inherit my gold
rings and car keys when quick as a wink
I go where I go with nothing to hold

but my own hands. I wish I were bold
I wish I could love my old self and just sink.
Look, I said, look, we're old now, we're old
I go where I go with nothing to hold.

ELAINE MINTZER

Elaine Mintzer was born in Los Angeles, and lived most of her childhood in the San Fernando Valley. After a year abroad, she got degrees in English and Education at cross-town rival schools UCLA and USC. She still lives in the suburbs of Los Angeles with her husband, two children, and a variety of pets. She has had work published in a number of magazines, including *ONTHEBUS, Spillway, Cold-drill, Rohwedder, Pearl, Shiela-na-gig,* and *West/Word*. Ms. Mintzer wrote poetry for, and read with the dance performance in Miami Beach of the dance company, Ballet Randolph. She has recently returned to teaching.

FOR WHAT AILS YOU

I cook a soup
with russets and sweet potatoes,
onions, carrots, parsley and garlic
boiled together with salt.
Salt is the key.
Salt to soothe a reddened throat.
Salt to bathe sore membranes.

I wash myself in the broth.
Pour it in my ear.
Draw it into my bowels.
Cook and season my innards,
to hide in the stuffing
the offal we throw away:
liver, heart, gizzard,
grief, anger, regret.

UNMENDED FENCE

Don't be neighbors with a dead man
whose retaining wall, yellowed
and dark-cracked like his teeth,
juts into my yard and pushes
earth and roots against our common edge.

He was dead before he died:
left deaf and spiritless by his old wife
who was swallowed by her own last cry,
not quite dead,
her voice for months muffled
under the wild ivy
and scraggly junipers,
easy to neglect
and difficult to tame...

And when she finally went, he got quiet.
No radio. No TV.
No singing in the shower.

No shower.
No washing.
No water.
Just the wait for her
to end this argument
and come up for air.
That's how they found him,
after some days:
ripe, and cock-eyed
with expectation.

Now there is no one for me to rail against
about the tilting of this wall.
My children and I mow our lawn,
pick snails, play freeze tag
under the shadow of a speculator's tidal wave
of new palms, poinsettia, and bougainvillea
poised on the horizon and ready to break
black-edged block and grain
over my head, and my children's,
spilling into our shoes
and under our flimsy clothes
till we relax from this task
of holding back the earth
and lie back under its slow lean.

FOR THE DEATH OF THEIR UNION

Their aging house stands intact, condemned.
Its matted carpets are unseamed.
Where the mirror adhered to the wall
gummed splotches turn to rust.
The recyclables have been thrown away.

Even before the hammering began
the marriage splintered.
By final inspection
she couldn't remember his smile.

The husband has a pinched schoolmaster's tolerance,
a basset's muscled pace.
He is determined to maintain
his dour dedication to pain.

He is off the mark. He revels
in history's inevitable perverse drive
to repeat itself.
He never considered insurrection
from the bow-lipped family
in their framed perfection
nailed by a cross-taped paneling nail
too weak for the weight
of this endeavor.

When his wife breaks with him
it is Mother's face he smashes.
An army of statistics,
the mildewed decrees of divorce
in leaky storage and forgotten letters
texture memories newly reconstructed.

The memories of bouncy girls
with their love for men
who in reality sag more motherly now;
thick-waisted
they burn over stoves
and figure calories and cream sauce.

He wanted only love.
No demands.
No children.
No edifice to be shared.

Demolition is soon.
Commitment of all the money.
In town, the bank holds the paper,
owns the old house
and the new.
The dream and the reality.

And when his wife leafs through the bills,
the numbers of construction and divorce
balance and parallel.

Once they thought this house could make them happy.
They flirted
with fantasy babies
swimming in endless summer aqua.

Now the husband stands at the back fence,
trying to see through to the water.
With his left hand, he thumbs
the keys around a key ring.
He bends down to pull a dandelion,
but leaves it in the flower bed.
Their house is gone.
Attorneys, like barracuda,
circle the bloody pool.

STIGMA

My mother called me Margarita,
an optimistic name for a daisy
that grows abundantly and well
in containers for several years.
She didn't think about the fact
that flowers give their whole lives
for a creep above the damp concrete;
then fall, practically invisible.
And after they are spent,
they are easy to replace.

We are given names that encourage sunny dispositions, control and good
manners: Rose. Lily.
Or names that speak of ancestral landscapes
and fragrance: Heather. Jasmine.
Even Iris, for our sexual proclivities
(our mothers' desires
that we grow beautiful,

but never free and wild,
never Dandelion, never Poppy).
We camouflage the asymmetries
with makeup and foundations,
because we love the smooth,
call perfect the unblemished
and accept too late
our own scars,
tattoos,
experiences.

So I wear my losses like a leper:
a sister has taken my right hand
my baby took a knee,
a kind of calcium depletion;
and I am incomplete.

My lover checks out the neighbor in short-shorts
pulling two panting beagles on tight leashes.
"Look at the bougainvillea," he tells me
while he is looking at her,
"the way the petals fade clear
and papery."

I want his eye and his hand,
not just the name of our relationship.
I am transparent with this lack
of attention.   And under
my lacy dress, I swear
I am stony and real as bone,
as real as any body.

ALL LIES

I hate to watch the flow of blood.
I hate the red against skin
and the way hairs and freckles become incidental.
The way things happen just by accident
and blood becomes everything.

I think Gunther belongs to me.
I keep him in my closet,
my sister's dog,
his boneless body with white floppy ears.
I will never let my sister have him back.

"He is mine now," I tell her.
"Go to hell," I tell her.
"You left him and he is mine," I tell her.
All the things she did
and thought, and loved,
they are mine.
I keep them all.
All the things my sister gave to me
and all the things she didn't.

I keep her children who would never be born.
I keep her fortieth birthday.
I keep the last sixteen candles
from her last birthday cake.
I keep her yellow nightgown.
I keep her Judy Collins album.
I keep her broken-backed copy
of *Little Women* she borrowed from me
and never gave back.
I keep the people she loved
who loved her.
She was so selfish.
Everyone always said that about her
and not about me...how she saved every nickel.

I hate her
and the blood going nowhere in her brain,
the long wait all day
and half the night
in the hospital lobby
where Cal Worthington came in
without his rows of used cars,
without his dog Spot.

I wish for her to be dead.
And for me to keep her brain
and her dog, and a picture she made in 7th grade.
Now I will put all her nickels in my bank.
Save up for a teddy bear.
One with more stamina than Gunther,
who'd already given up.
One who will not just lie there
limp and glassy-eyed.

HARVEST

In our motel room
we are five in a row in beds
made up green
and orange like the new
toothbrushes we had to buy
having forgotten our own

back home. Four of us read
and one child pouts, clapping hands
on her belly, unable to fall asleep,
buzzing with all this light
and talk and expectation
of tomorrow's trip.

She's hungry she says.
I put down my book,
pat the bed beside me.
She squeezes in next to me,
presses her head against my shoulder,
wiggles for a moment.
I am enough for her,
and I have enough

because I have hoed the past into my garden:
compost, leaf meal and sisters
spaded in and well watered.
Nitrogen, phosphorous , potassium,

missed children and bellies only fat,
not pregnant. A rich blend.
I plant lettuce and squash.
Corn by the south wall
and cauliflower near the garage.
And seeds for flowers.
Some sprout, some don't.

Weeds, for sure.
Oh, the weeds, for sure.

MAIZE

Corn with a woman's name
lies decorative and dry
in my basket, a basket
woven like kernels,
at once rough and smooth,
its job merely ornamental
now, not functional. Women
do not age that way. Oh yes,

our teeth go black and spaced,
our skin feels like feathers
in spite of the ridges.
But no one peels back
our clothes and discards them
husk-like on the floor.
And our fruit is hard and pithy
as advice often is.

Now we wait on tables
for another season,
for a time to sit again
among the rows of corn,
in the green and spiky leaves,
silk tassels gold and red
waving in the wind for water,
enough to quench our thirsts.

GRAVID

It's the end of May and all the mothers are heavy
with morning fog and endless trips
to school and baseball.
We know that heat will follow.
It will be a different kind of hell
of no respite from the kids;
of baking walls and soles burning
on the blacktop.

At the end of May we are ripe too early,
and greet each other with perfunctory hellos
and yell, impatient with the children
who beg for one more zipper
or shoelace or barrette to be fastened,
for ice cream and cookies and candy
but we offer only fresh fruit and they complain
as we drop things because our hands
are so full, so full of mother,
the mother always inside,
the mother talking
till we want to spit ourselves out.
She says she will take care of me.
But she leaves no room,
because I am too big and pithy—
mealy as a bitten apple
left to ferment on the ground.

We had a tree in the backyard.
Every summer, it bore only a few apricots,
mostly out of reach on the top branches.
One or two fell off,
bird-pecked and smeared with droppings.
Mom washed them carefully,
cut away the ragged hole,
cut it smooth and shiny and wet.
It's all right, she says.
I cut away the bad spot.

The birds know, she says,
which are the sweetest.

HOUSEWORK

Hear the buzz of children
where golden-tailed pheasants
rise blind from the sofa
and leave me nothing
but horizontal dust.

Loose change jangles
in my folds and crevices.

Philodendrons and spider plants
in their own struggle
between gravity and air
hide the dirt
in spider-infested corners.

I am tired of the vacuum.
This ritual of withdrawal
leaves me thoughtless, eyeless,
and visible only to those blood-sucking
gnats and mosquitos.
My torso sticks to the carpet
because there is no reason
for perpendicular.

And all the time, those stiff-winged
insects light on my palms,
swaggering in their egocentric ways.

ROOTLESS

There is a greenhouse
in an industrial park in Gardena,
where they grow tillandsia: bromeliads.
Laborers glue the thick-leaved and rootless plants

to gnarled chunks of Northern California grape wood,
one hundred-year-old vines
sold by the truck-load
then sawed into lengths
and rumbled around for days
in a cement truck
to knock off all the bark
leaving a sculpture of excrement-colored wood,
perfect base for these imported beauties;
the owner says Florida airplants are too hard to cultivate.

Carol found a tree frog.
One gray inch of earth history
amid the cycads and staghorn ferns.
She wants a new staghorn.
The owner tells us
staghorn ferns don't pup.
He picks up a frog.
One that was immersed in pesticide.
The owner washes him off
and watches as he develops the asymmetry
of loss of muscle control,
coordination, direction.
A shower doesn't help.
Carol says a frog in the greenhouse
is a sign of ecological health,
that the world-wide frog population
is diminishing and they don't know why.
I know why.
It is because they have lost their direction.
They want to be beautiful
but don't know how.
Some die for wanting.

Some go out and get jobs.
And some ride the leaves of the staghorn,
jump and crawl in the moss
and grass and heat and humidity.

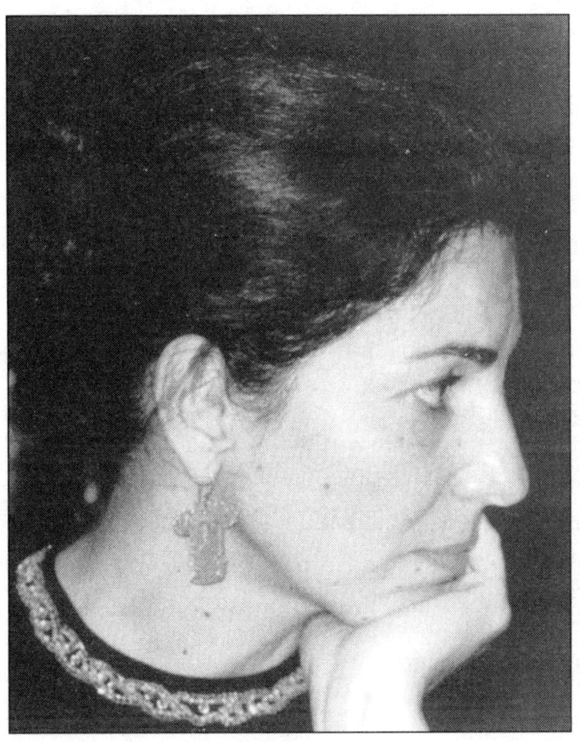

GILLA NISSAN

Gilla Nissan was born in Tel Aviv, Israel and has lived in Los
Angeles since 1974. She studied Art History and Philosophy at
Tel Aviv University. In Los Angeles, she graduated from
Yeshiva University West Coast Teacher Seminar and continued
to the University of Judaism, where she recieved her bachelor's
degree in Modern Hebrew Literature and Jewish Studies. She is
the author of five chap books including *Powdered Light* and *All
That Space*. Her work has been published in *ONTHEBUS*,
Spillway, and other literary journals and newsletters. In 1993
she won first prize in the Miriam Felicia Lindberg Israel Poetry
Peace Prize for the poem "On the Sixth Day."

BATMAN IS DEPRESSED

The truth is that during the last seven years
I rarely watched T.V.,
but yesterday my kids hopped into my bed
and suggested sweetly to turn it on.
and I always try to measure resistance wisely
so I said, "O.K."
They said, "Cool,"
and we all wrapped up together.
Batman was there
delivering his usual life story.

The truth is that he seemed depressed
and run-down; he was tired of all that,
he couldn't take it anymore,
I mean let's face it—
he tried for many years to do the same thing
and everybody believed in him
and he believed in him,
now he knows
he couldn't save the world anymore.
"Batman is depressed," I murmured.
"Come on, Mommy,
we want to have a nice time."
"Sorry," I said and pulled myself together.
Here come the commercials.
I haven't seen those for a while.
Ooo la la! What a new level,
so much more sophisticated,
must be "special" for Christmas.
I could see tons of money and work
poured into them: the superb music,
the images, the feelings evoked.
I could see the best people working on them,
New Age people,
artists who are trained spiritually, no doubt,
people who have nothing to do with the end product,
people who will never take
Alka Seltzer, aspirin, or soda pop,

who are just offering their services to the "real" big people
who are democratically cheating the masses
and legally keeping them numb
in a relatively semi-comfortable system.

Just open up, feel yourself, release tension,
feel the beyond, be more than your limitations
go further, touch real beauty,
have a perfect body, a perfect machine,
perfect harmony, more energy
and let us tell you how.
All you need to do is:
first, of course, drink Coca Cola,
then wear Kukuriku panty hose,
use Sha-la-la perfume,
and step into a Toyota,
which was all you wished for
all your life,
but you just weren't in touch with it.
We bring you in touch with what you asked for
and now you got it—Toyota.
And don't go anywhere,
we'll be right back.

I looked at my little Daniel
and felt that I had fed him
rotten apples.
But he seemed content.

I remember a wise man's comment,
that there is
a real holocaust happening
all the time, right here and now.
And we don't even see it.

LONG HALLWAY

My daughter is back
from a long trip.
She missed me so much.
"It's good to be home," she said,
taller than ever,
soft and certain about herself.
I watched her body growing
in front of my eyes, now and now.
"Mom, I'm almost as tall as you."
I feel almost relieved.
Maybe I do not need
to be tall anymore,
to carry the flag of who I am.
I am a mom,
the flag carries me.
When I go back to myself,
I need to walk
a long hallway
to get to a room
with no walls,
a balcony overlooking the mom,
the woman, the speechless poet,
the untitled me.

FROM RED TO GREEN

I stop at a red light,
and a tall black guy, pleasant,
stands next to me
but far away,
with a sign that says: "Need work."

How do I relate to him?
I open the window and ask,
"Do you have any work for me?"
"No," he replies kindly as if
he would give it to me if he had.
"Where are you from?" he asks.
That is always too deep of a question for me,
so I tell him I was born in Israel.
"My name is Israel," he smiles.
And I smile too.
Green light.
I point my thumb up like Americans do for cool.
He makes a V with his fingers like winners do.

NON-BIODEGRADABLE

I was told the moon would be full
today at around noon;
the rivers will flood
the land,
my emotions
will mess up my life.
I got drops of flowers' essence
to cheer me up.
I went to a delicatessen store
and tried strange cheeses,
I bought a rug
which I will return tomorrow
when the moon
will come back to its senses.
My mother is still dead;
I just wanted her to hug my son.
I set it up so I will be rejected;

if the earth will reject me
like others do,
I will go straight to heaven.
Meanwhile I will put the shame
in plastic bags
and bury them in my body,
mark them "non-biodegradable."

MORE

The door is wide open
Soon Jonah will come out of its mouth,
does he really want to be here?
I was left behind like a security guard,
to watch over our lost garden.
Security is when you fly without a seatbelt
and flying is teasing and responding
magnetically to your love.
Love is a gold and purple silk road.
Magnetic is when I follow my heart
whenever it goes and sharing it with my mind
which sees without labeling any more.
More is just staying there,
being the waves, Jonah, blue, God,
the whale's solar plexus
the shore, the sin, being in and out in
and out
in and
out
the door.

JUST TO FALL

Now I return all the videos
on time
even if it's 10:30 at night
and the parking lot
has oil spots all over
and weird people are coming and going
and McDonalds is just there,
with all their junk food
and screaming lights,
it's just something I will not do:
leave home at 10:30 p.m.
and stand in an oily parking lot
and watch how people are different
at this hour of the night,
somehow careless about themselves and loud,
just near that ugly big yellow M
pretending to be a big mama
to shine upon the poor and hungry.
I hate it.
Still I come here,
hop over those oily spots,
black oily spots
with the yellow light in them
just to fall into your arms.

ON THE SIXTH DAY

Chopping Italian parsley fine,
I know I cannot
verbalize my life.
Soon angels of the seventh heaven
will shake powdered light over the city.
I smell the sauteed parsley and cilantro

with dry limes,
it's my mother circling with the angels,
to make a canopy of peace above me.
Soon when I stand in front of You
like candlesticks longing for Shabbat,
please put a garment of light on me,
for Your name.

POPPIES

You know those moments
when you notice someone
then you notice that you notice him
and then you just don't leave it at that
and you start to bring
more and more parts of yourself to it
and it's just not clear
where things are
and you see
that this space is actually
the love of your life
and actually the only one
which is the unlabeled one.
The rest can also be exciting
but you need to work for it
while this one has its own light
like the way the moon is different from the sun
because it does not have a light of its own.

IN A CERTAIN LIGHT

In a certain light the skin on my hands
looks really really worn out. You really
feel like taking off the gloves and just
be what you remember yourself to be,
hands that know less but look fresh and promising.
In a certain light the wrinkles of my mind
are trying to remember the names of flowers
I used to know in Hebrew and now do not know
in any language. Thank God things exist
with or without names. Like the way Bill and I
sat together in the canyon
just knowing that we are,
an existence which didn't care in particular
for a name—a connection which
was almost afraid of itself
and wanted to jump into a word.
But we didn't let it.

ALL THAT SPACE

What is the question
my life
is the answer for?
I must be
an answer
for a certain longing,
for a bow
which I made long ago.
What is it this morning
by my windows?
I am still and simple as I can be.
Tell me; make me see it,

since I have only one drop
of purple to cover
all that space.

THE KITCHEN

My mother and my grandmother
are not here.
But the way they do things is.
The way I hold the knife
and cut these strawberries,
is the way my grandmother
did and my mother too.
Now the time is gone.
My kitchen and theirs is one,
the same air.
This moment has all the wisdom
I need.
My life is a valley,
at my feet.

TO WATER THE TREES

I was only two and a half
when I asked Uncle Mushka
to let me water Grandma's fruit trees.
"When you'll be older," he said.
There, in Grandma's backyard,
in front of her doves watching us,
with the very mild wind
sweeping the air to the sea,
wafting all the market smells toward sunset,
very gently
as not to disturb

the silence
of the end of the day.

A PEACOCK

Adaya is my daughter.
She came and stood behind me,
under the yellow blossoms of our Acacia tree
while I was talking to Jack.
"My tail is here," I said with pleasure.
"I am not your tail," she said.
"It depends." I said, "What if I am a peacock?"

AVIVI

comes to the kitchen and says,
"My mom isn't here yet."
"But you are here," I say.
"But where is she?"
"She is where she is·
maybe sitting in her office
or going down the elevator
or in her car,
driving to come pick you up.
Who knows?
Did you notice
that people can only be
where they are?"

AT 3

Mommy, Mommy listen,
I can hear my own voice
"Hello!"
"Hello!"

IT IS GOOD

it is good for a man
in gardens
to sit
for a while
and slowly
or all at once
to know

A NAME

it's a holy place
can somebody hear me?
give me a name
and I will call it out.

JAMES O'HERN

JAMES O'HERN grew up on a ranch in Laredo, Texas on the border with Mexico. He attended Kemper Military School in Missouri, Southern Methodist University in Texas, and the New York University Graduate School of Business in New York City. For more than twenty years, Mr. O'Hern has been an investment banker and corporate executive in New York, London, and Los Angeles. He is married and maintains residences in Los Angeles and New York City.

THE POND

At the edge
Of a garden pond
I hear
The inaudible cry
Of tadpoles
As tiny whales speak

In my dark reflection
I see histories stacked
Beneath the surface
Like generations
Of an ancient city
Built upon itself

At the end of the summer
When water in the pond
Turns black
It is my job
To save the fish

As they drained
Dying water
To clean away the scum
I embrace and bundle
Slimy stalks
Of drooping lilies

Chase gold
And silver minnows
From catchment to catchment
Scoop them into buckets
With a kitchen sieve

When the pond is safe again
With an open hand
I lick the trembling hearts
Of scum-slickered minnows

And replace them
One by one
Into reborn waters
As I say a child's prayer

Hoping that one day
When my sky goes black
As the pool did that summer
One of them will remember

CHISPA

An old Indian named Chispa
a wetback in hiding
lived in an abandoned shack
on the south quarter near the river
on our ranch in South Texas

He was from Cerralvo
across the border in Mexico
said he was pure Coahuiltecan
the tribe who once claimed this land

Once or twice a month
I bought groceries for him
flour beans fresh vegetables
salt pork Clamente Jacques jalapenas
with no stuffing of cheese or fish

On the days I came with food
he fixed a menudo-like stew
cooking it down to a hot red oily stock
then added hominy vegetables and bits of meat
from the small game he shot
served it with tortillas de harina
canned jalapenas and fresh chilipiquines

that would raise a blister
if the juice touched a lip

After lunch we sat out behind the shack
on a slope overlooking the river
that in summer was only a stream
with the sun hot overhead
nothing moved except rainbows of heat
'plumas de fuego' that stood on end
and danced between us and the river

We talked mostly in Spanish
but when he told a story
he would often lapse into Nahautl
and still I understood his words
and what he taught me about dreams
mostly the ones about animals
and how to get inside their skin

He taught me to call quail
by blowing ocarina notes
through my thumb knuckles
and call up rutting bucks
with a doe's wail bleated out
on a mesquite carved cacto-reed

But the hardest of all to fool
were the coyotes he said
those wily brothers
with whom he shared a totem soul

To get past their cunning
I became the victim itself and
from the edge of a child's voice
released the high pitched scream
of a dying rabbit

When the rabbit is caught
in the jaws of its predator
it sings three songs

First it cries out in alarm
warning others not to come this way

Then as fangs rip through flesh
pain gives out a scream of terror

The last notes to be heard
are like the weeping of a child

As prey grants permission
to its predator

ROCK SOUP

At our ranch in Zapata, on the Mexican border, it was
the peak of summer. Only a single caretaker was on hand
to sustain the few head of Brahma and Longhorn leftover
between seasons. Not much work was done during that
period and some days got so hot everything stopped.

On one of those days, Chispa put a rusty iron pot on the
wood stove, stoked it with mesquite and began making
soup. He poured water from a clay jug balanced on his
hip. Then added greens, onions, peppers and fresh
tomatoes I brought from the market. The turnips and
long white radishes came from his garden-patch out back.
Then he took out an old wooden box lined with a
parchment and pinched out a palm of red dirt. He asked
me to taste it and put some in the pot. Said it was magic
clay for rock soup.

While the pot boiled, we went outside to the shade of a
lean-to looking out over the shimmer of dirt fields at the
dying river below. Fields where we had planted cedar
fence posts until my hands bled. Strung barbed wire as
tight as any piano. Those two quarter-acre fields waiting
for water from a tank with a dam that had yet to be fixed.

And, the fields still needing a full season of rain before
we could plant sorghum.

The sun is overhead almost now to the point of no shade.
Everything is asleep but us. No noise except for the
droning of cicadas. We wait in the buzzing silence... wait
for the moment when rainbows rise... fluttering on end...
draining color from the empty fields. Suddenly the
cicadas stop... hanging on a high note. Now I can only
hear the fluttering... a headache coming on... sunstroke or
hunger... I can't tell...

Chispa gets up, motions it is time to start the hunt. Bare
to the waist and without guns, we begin stalking, first in
the creek beds. Scanning under scrub brush, we squint at
shadows that shouldn't be there, study rocks, alert to a
quiver or blink... suddenly Chispa is airborne. I follow,
hurdling full speed over brush, chasing the cottontail out
not from behind, or under a big rock but, the rock itself
came alive, now bounding away and us following
broken-field, sidestepping, vaulting over up and through,
jerk to a halt as the rabbit slows... my temples pound,
sweat streams down, burning my eyes, tasting like my
own blood...then we go again, flushing him to the next
spot — seven times: the running, flushing, stopping —
until finally he winds down, stops under a scrub —
gasping, gagging, then shows us a tiny pink tongue and ...
Chispa walks over and gently picks him up by the ears.

He hands me the rabbit to carry back to the shack.
Cradled quiet in my arms, I feel his heart whir against my
chest. Inside, Chispa lifts the rabbit by the ears again,
stretching him lengthwise over the pot as I hold his legs.
Then, he slits the rabbits throat letting its hot blood pour
out into our soup.

There is a time in the Mexican desert when nothing
moves. No living thing quivers, twitches or crawls, not
even to save itself. This happens as the sun falters, as
rivers stop to make big loops in the mud and, if you look
up, the shadows have gone. For a moment, everything
waits for the sun to move for the earth to bleed
That is the moment

when everything becomes possible.

At least, that is the way I remember it.

RACOON

Every night at dinner
me still in a high chair
my father's eyes would stalk mine
ready to root out disobedience
even before it became a thought

That's when I learned to disappear

I started hunting when I was seven
killed my first buck that year
One day I got bored hunting deer
so I stalked a rabbit
following him to a watering hole

I saw what looked like a bear
ambling along the edge of the lake
but it was a big racoon
bobbing and weaving
rising up on his haunches
then down into a traveling slouch
fishing along the bank for breakfast

As he came closer I snuck up
to corner him on a narrow point
that jutted from shore

Every time he looked up
I swayed with the brush
and sucked down into myself
until I disappeared

With my gun at ready
I moved in
and when I was right behind
revealed myself to him with a hiss

He reeled around to face me
locked his eyes to mine
then sprung out to full height

He stood his ground staring
I began to tremble
then put down my gun
and stepped aside
to give him room to pass

which he did with great dignity

JOB'S APOLOGY

*Who is this whose ignorant words
cover my design with darkness?*
                    The Book of Job

What do you want of me?

I know I have offended you and now
have the task of pleasing you
while staying true to myself
I tremble in the face of your power
and know that what I know is nothing
but perhaps a fleck at most a pittance
in the shadow of your truth
and yet somewhere inside this skinny body
this self created by you out of thin air
which will rot before your very eyes
this figment of your whim and upon whose mercy
my very breath depends for each heave and sigh

somewhere inside this pond of body scum
is a lily pad that does not sink beneath my weight
one on which if I stand in its palm and stay I will be safe
Not safe from your wrath or beyond its pain
but stand enfolded in the calm of its center
a knowing of not knowing — a seeing of not seeing
beyond even the ultimate reach of your benevolent pity
and if I speak from this place
what form what words will please you to listen
what will stop you to hear what I say
and why should you listen since you must already know
whatever I might think to think or even dare to say
but there is one thing or maybe two at most
to which you are not
            — will I be struck down as I say this? —
to which you cannot be the ultimate authority

> *how I feel in the face of death*
> *and what I see behind your back*

BUFFALO

Three buffalo tumble
from the edge of a cliff

When I saw this picture
in the entertainment section
of the Sunday Times
I had to put the paper down
and go out for a walk

It is foggy this morning
I see a profusion of flowers
in the center dividers
along Avenue of the Stars

It is a pretty boulevard
but I'm thinking
how a boulevard in Century City
is different than one in Paris
or even New York
Here you don't see many people
walking and enjoying themselves

I wonder why even the flowers
seem fake this morning and
why I'm so upset about buffalo

Of all the violence
we see in the media every day
pictures of bloody babies
stories about AIDS Ebola
homicide genocide suicide terror
in every corner of the globe
I wonder why I feel afraid
why I can't let go of the image
of those three tumbling buffalo

Then I remember what I was told
by a well-known poet
at a writer's conference last summer

He said I should not attribute
so many human qualities to animals
when I write about them

But here I am doing it again
I am wondering how *they* felt
the buffalo
not the people who used the picture
to promote a U-2 album
not the ones who took the picture
or the ones who caused the stampede
and watched as the earth fell
out from under them

No what I'm wondering about
is why I feel so unsafe
living here in Century City
right here on Avenue of the Stars
across from 20th Century Fox
in this the City of Angels
where five million other people live
usually safely with each other
and I'm not worried about AIDS
or Ebola and as far as I know
killer bees haven't crossed the border yet
and we haven't had a riot or an earthquake
for more than a year

HEARING RAIN

Today is Easter Sunday
5 AM and it's raining

I didn't notice the rain
until after I poured my tea
returning twice to the kettle
to see why it didn't shut off

I thought it was the kettle
but it was the rain I heard
coming down on slanted glass
of the garden room next door

When I saw my mistake
I felt a shiver of fear
thinking I'd been caught
doing something shameful

Then the sadness came

as I saw how far I've gone
from the part of me
that understands the intentions of rain

SANCUDO

Whenever Chispa saw me hurt or about to cry
he would put his arms around me from behind and would say:

Sancudo, no lloras
estoy aqui con tigo
and I knew everything was going to be all right

Sancudo means little mosquito
that buzzes around in the night
drinking blood and dodging swats
and growing up to be a buzzard
or an eagle

JAN RUCKERT

JAN RUCKERT is a psychologist, artist and writer. Her poems have appeared in *ONTHEBUS*, *Blood Pudding*, *Voices* and *Spillway*. Her books include *The Four-Footed Therapist: How Your Pet Can Help You Solve Your Problems*, and *Are You My Dog: How To Find Your Best Friend*, published by Ten Speed Press. She lives in Los Angeles with her two Rottweilers, Delilah and Cachet.

NEW PAINT

From my white couch
I see the rusted pipes in the atrium.
They're covered with red primer to prevent corrosion.
They're ready for paint they say will last five years.
I love the clean look that promises new surfaces.

The driveway lost those big potholes
where cars stuttered up the grade,
the kitchen cupboards have been caulked
where the yellow showed through
from the paint over twenty-five years old,
and the gates where two dogs broke through
are soon to be redwood.

I don't want to forget
all the changes in the house.
This morning when I clipped
the play review for Michael
I thought about the chipping paint
about cream that shines a little in the sunlight,
or soft white texture that weaves its way into drapes
when the redwood gates smell woody
and look so strong they will open easily
and close to protect me.

INTIMACY

My friend tells me she is falling in love
with a guy she met at Great Expectations.
She got this membership on sale
thirteen hundred dollars
for life.
Out of six request cards
he is the only one who says yes.
They talk for three hours on the phone

and then they meet—
That's the interview.
He's an actor in some theater production,
does bit parts in film,
cowboy stuff with Clint Eastwood—
she worries if they have a family
can he support the kids,
will she have to work the rest of her life.
I remind her she's only known him a week
but she says
he's the first one who talks to her
like a person
and the therapist he's been seeing for seven years
says he's ready for intimacy.
I think about the price of intimacy
the thirteen hundred dollars she paid to choose
the right guy
and as I watch the leaves fall on my driveway,
the days grow shorter,
I wonder how long it lasts
in a falling market.

GATEWAY 2000

This love-hate business has gone on
for as long as I can remember.
When I first saw his screen—larger than most—
print styles the old-fashioned way,
I could feel my heart beat,
my eyes get blurry.
I wanted to say yes right away
but the desire to look cool prevailed,
so I reached over and moved his mouse
slowly, across the board,
touched it in a gentle way with the end of my fingers,
no time to be weak,
I crawled up on the desk,

put my legs around the edge of the disc.
Then he started asking questions about what I wanted . . .
of course, that old shyness came back
the keys all looked the same
I was afraid it might be over
but he just kept offering options,
memory slots for anything.
When I dropped the mouse and reached for him,
his wires drew me in
and there was his name
Gateway 2000 IDE Host Adapter.
It was a scalable font
so I disappeared right into the screen.

We formatted for hours under the green light,
didn't have to convert a document—
just disc to disc.
It was simultaneous transfer all the way.
The next time you turn it on,
there I am,
the right connections already built in
all you have to do is put an arrow on me and click.

A SIMPLE DESIGN

The one who thought he could
improve my poetry by taking me to bed,
now worries I may be losing my edge.
You can never win with a man.
They start by trying to move you closer
to where they are,
closer so you will listen to what they think,
which they rarely say quickly,
closer to their bed,
where you will discover
something about them
they have forgotten.

I would prefer lust to love
you know what you have,
something you can taste
and hold in your hand,
no discussion about tomorrow,
what he thinks of you,
when he will call,
does he mean what he says
and who else is he saying it to.

Just clean lines,
a simple design
no fuzzy watercolors
waiting on the page.

TO JOHN BERRYMAN

Forgive another letter so soon on the heels of the last one
but with the holidays coming, I won't be writing for awhile.
I jog through them, just like you,
homesick for a home we never had.

I have never been able to figure the formula
for spending and saving
that equals the value of life.
You can save money but your days are spent
and your years have a minus at the end.
I read somewhere you were always short of money,
teaching contracts from years to year, begging foundation funds.
I think about growing old and not having enough money to live.
I try to estimate the figures for a budget
but I don't know how many years to save for,
how long it will be then.
I read an article with helpful tips:
secure your future,
avoid early withdrawal,
ladder your maturities,

spend less by cocooning.
I think about your early withdrawal
into cold water where you had no chance to reinvest,
how you turned your back on it.
You just chose a figure: 58 years
no more salary worries,
no more fear of bad reviews,
the weak muse voice,
just,
"This is it."
I picture you standing there in January,
cold against a metal railing,
thinking about your balance,
what penalties for this act,
what credit lost.

I have chosen the age of 85.
My mother died at 76,
my father over 80,
and life expectancy
since you left
keeps increasing.

When I think about you and your friends,
pub-crawl sanity,
fear of becoming verse-barren
I wonder,
did you dip into your bodies,
your wives,
for poems;
dig up slices of word-flesh,
slosh it all with alcohol?
You just let it all come in on you, John,
like a sea storm.

Well, what I wanted to tell you was
I'm sorry you didn't stay longer,
that you didn't look through those glasses
you kept in your shoes at night,
to see winds blow your wail-shadows away.

If you had come to visit me,
you and Henry could have slept
on the blue futon in my back room.
Sure, it's cold this month,
but I would close the doggie door
to keep the draft out,
push up the heater
and lend you my oldest dog
to protect you.
No bad spirits can ever get past her.
In the morning you could slip out
into the yard,
walk with the squirrels,
fill the birdbath and watch the quail.
I'd cut the variegated roses that still bloom in winter,
arrange them on your bathroom counter,
and when I returned from walking dogs,
I'd make us vanilla bean coffee,
toasted bagels with my cousin's peach preserves.
You could teach me all you know,
and since I read somewhere
that you were careful about your weight,
I'd make you my favorite recipe from *Sunset Magazine*
the sugarless apple pie,
and we could read the poet friends you used to know,
cocoon a little while I teach you
how to make your dream songs sweet again.

HER POOL, HER GUY, HER JEST

The pool is spooked.
This is a nightspot,
wanna strip? Then why not.
He's one of those guys
that Sexy Sally likes to watch
take off his towel,
over the edge those long legs

kick away the leaves on top,

frog it all free under the surface.
He makes a big deal about going in—
in winter, the colder the better,
as if his thermostat can turn it all on.
Watch me, the universal boy cry—
touch me,
here.
She's not used to this at all.

Sexy Sally forgets tired bones, forgets coyotes
that eat their prey,
forgets the warning hoot of owls
perched in the redwood trees.
She wants to keep up the pace
of frosty-whip steam,
wants to ride the night spot.
I think she got a hot one tonight.

THE SECRET

Two crows perch
on the redwood that is dying
in my backyard.

I read biologists increase the life span
of translucent worms
no bigger than a printed comma,
molecular white-coated men
who play with hormones,
trace mice cells,
search for the pill in yeast,
a storage place of brain messages
to stop our dying.
They gather in laboratories
like some once sat in churches,

pray for cellular senescence,
talk about chromium that helps
an elderly fruit fly mate later,
a rat live one third longer,
offer their advice on protein
to preserve the memory of a gerbil.

I am amazed that all this could happen.
That if my dog and I were born today
we might live twice as long.
I think of my father
wanting me to sip flaxseed tea,
telling me, I should drink
six glasses of water daily,
walk the dogs, breath deep,
be courteous and fair.
Because he knew all this and lived past eighty,
did he know something I can do now,
a secret
I can teach my friends, my dog
something I can put in the bed
of the redwood
to call the tree
to life.

HEALTH WAVES

I wait for my knee to heal
and search for an acupuncturist who will carry me
into the valley of health
with needles.

A shaky Chinese voice on the telephone
tells me herb tea costing $10
will clear my body
and allow the energy to flow.

My friend recommends a woman
whose suite has three rooms,
where she puts three bodies,
needles in each one.
If you want her to stay with you,
you pay extra.
When I call my insurance company,
a voice they warn is monitored,
informs me that payment for this service
requires proof
that it will change your condition.

I make myself a cup of herb tea
and think about my vessels,
how they will open themselves
to ancient medicine,
to this wise, small woman
far more patient than I am,
who has some secret way
to talk to bones,
to seduce this stiff knee into a love dance,
into a peaceful alliance,
health in our time.
I take another bitter sip,
think about polarities,
the I-Ching and the wise one
who waits for the mountain to speak,
for the waters to return
to the mouth of the people.

WITHOUT SEASON

For the past week,
my friend's dog in heat whimpers,
and the other dog,
an older male, howls,
places love nips on her muzzle,
sniffs the familiar scent,

longs for the placement of his part
inside that open part of hers.
She paces, moves in front of him
raises her rear, believing
he will remember.
Kibble and crunchy rawhide chews
cannot stop her moon look,
the droop ears,
blood drops that mark the rug.
But he is almost ten,
old for his breed,
and when he tries to mount,
falls off.

Because no one in that house can sleep at night
he comes to stay with me, here,
where my female dog lives without season.
On the floor beneath my bed
they lie on separate pillows,
nuzzle just a little before the lights go out.
I arrange my own pillows,
turn up the blanket on my bed,
then, just before the snores,
wonder if they remember
their bodies together,
the long tie,
the thrust of younger years.

PATRICIA L. SCRUGGS

PATRICIA L. SCRUGGS is a Colorado native who grew up in Alberta, Canada. She earned her BA and MFA at California State University, Fullerton. A long-time resident of Southern California, Scruggs teaches high school art. She is married, has two grown children and one grandson. Her work has been in *Voices, onTarget, West/Word, Mosaic, Spillway, ONTHEBUS, Second Glance,* and two anthologies, *Women and Death* and *News From Inside.*

OREGON COAST

Two slender rock formations
rise from the sea
as if they belong together—
Yin and Yang.
I want them joined
by red ropes
as the Japanese do.

This long strand of seaweed
makes a marriage of sorts—
the rocks, the seaweed, me.
The next wave sweeps
my rope away.

Cold water slams
against my thighs
and reminds me
the tide is rising.

Trouble is,
I want too much
from this place,
and soon, I will
be gone from here.

MEASURING THE ARCH FOR MY MURAL

I stand under the ladder
and hold it steady
as my husband lowers the plumb.
"Now, reach out and stop its movement.
Tell me if it's on the mark," he says.
"A little to the left," I say.
The cold wind makes me
glad I wore my jacket.

He marks the line with a chalk
and begins to climb down.
The rungs of the ladder
frame his shoes.
I see them every day—
in the closet,
beside his desk,
under the bed.
Sensible brown shoes
worn so often,
they mimic his wide feet.

But, slightly above eye level,
these familiar shoes
surprise me.
They seem vulnerable.
I hold the ladder steady
as they carry my husband
to the solid ground.

FULL CIRCLE

My daughter, pregnant,
has lost the hollows
in her cheekbones,
gained breasts and hips.
She carries
her stomach
before her, proudly,
the way she carried
her pot belly
when she
was a toddler.

FINGERLINGS

Mosquito larvae float
on the surface of the pond.
My sister plans
to pour kerosene over them.
"Wait," my brother says,
"You'll kill the tadpoles."

He telephones fish stores.
No one has mosquito fish.
My brother drives from store to store
asking for fish that won't eat tadpoles,
finally decides to try goldfish.
He buys one hundred fingerlings
in two plastic bags.
Five-year-old Danny
helps put them in the pond.

Outside the house
where our mother
waits for death,
we gather
morning and afternoon
to count the fish,
the tadpoles,
watch the surface clear.

PORTRAITS

In a formal portrait,
the lady sits in a high-backed chair,
hands folded in lap,
staring pitilessly into the camera.
Her husband stands behind her,

ramrod straight,
one hand resting proprietarily
on the back of her chair,
while he takes care not to tilt his head
because it would put his mustache
at too rakish an angle.
Neither of them dare smile.

The small brown suitcase,
given to me by the wife
of my father's cousin,
contains portraits
or our dark-haired Griffith ancestors,
always in their Sunday best.
There are no names written on the backs.
The cardboard folders
identify the studio and city:
Shultz and Sons, Deadwood, South Dakota;
Brown's Portraits, Billings, Montana;
The Fuller Studio, Sheridan, Wyoming.

My sister bends over these faces,
studies them for clues.
She wants to know
their names, their stories.
If they died with any love
left over, she wants it.
She wants to claim their unused love.

NO ONE HEARS

In my dream I sail
on a 70 foot yacht,
the kind wealthy people own,
with my husband as the pilot.
We are part of a big group,
going to dinner at Woody's Wharf,

sailing over a sea of crayon blue.
As we watch dolphins
surf our wake, suddenly
the boat hits a reef and sinks.

One by one, we bob up and wade to shore.
My husband's parents haven't surfaced.
I go back, search the wreck,
find them in a topside cabin bunk,
their arms around each other,
peaceful, covered by water.
They could have waded ashore,
but they chose to die together.
My mother-in-law, who couldn't swim,
taped her mouth, so she wouldn't
cry out while drowning.

I hold them to my breast—
wet, the size of dolls,
their smiles like Kewpies.
"They want to be buried
in the same grave," I say.
But no one hears me.
The other passengers turn away,
walk toward candle light,
toward abalone and wine,
toward the sound of a slide trombone.

BLUE IRIS UNFOLDS

It has rained
for fourteen days,
but last night
I woke to see the moon
make a path of light
on the bay.

Today the sun breaks through
and I sit cross-legged
on the windowseat
absorbing warmth.
An open book of poems
rests on my thighs.

Two seals bob near the dock.
Pelicans fly past,
so low, their wings
almost touch the water.
A blue iris unfolds
on the dresser.

We've come together
for a long weekend,
my three friends and I.
Downstairs, laughter pops
over a champagne cork.
On a day like this,
I will live forever.

NARROW, THE SKY

Standing Woman grooves the base of the willow
into thirds, holds one part in her teeth
while her hands split it lengthwise.
"Pauite women," she says, "are not allowed
to make baskets until they are fifty."

She holds up a section, says,
"The wide end is the earth;
the narrow, the sky."
She picks up her knife.
"Cut the earth to a point.
Sky is the center of your coil.
Earth becomes a needle,
an instrument of creation."

On our way home that night
from the workshop in Yosemite,
Debbie's stereo blasts "Ave Maria."
I've always wanted to sing on key.
If I were a bird, I'd be a Meadowlark.

Debbie asks me questions I can't hear
while she drives 75 up the Grapevine.
"What's wrong?" she says.
"The temperature light came on.
I've never had it do that before!
What should I do?"
"Turn the heater on." I tell her.
She does, and also turns the volume up.
Just before we find our freeway exit,
we are both conducting
"The Ride of the Valkyries."

I thought when I turned forty,
wisdom would cover me like a basket.
And there we were, in Yosemite,
in a tiny, fenced enclosure,
unable to see the mountains,
learning to make them.

WATER

covers the town,
covers the land,
covers the cows
that graze in the fields,
their black ears wet, ruffled.
Ducks with fish heads
swim above them.

A little girl slides
down the bank
and into the water.

I dive in after her,
grab hold of her hand
but she kicks away,
swims toward the town.
I lose her
in a forest of cow's ears.

I try to climb the bank which becomes
the walls and fireplace of my mother's home.
The ceiling forces me to turn back.
I walk through the town
among strangers,
until a shopkeeper
who is not my mother says,
"Welcome, come in and be warm."

I lie down and sleep.
When I wake,
the moon is in the room.
My husband sleeps beside me.
I am the stranger here.

ELECTRIC JUNE

Today the girls wear shorts,
unwind legs that stretch forever,
pose idly, bend over the seated boys,
their long hair brushes the desktops,
young breasts push their tee shirts.

Poppycock. Get your fanny off the table.
Sit firm in your chair.
Sketch something. Draw flowers.
Stop vamping the glorious guys.

Just write what comes in the long, hot afternoon

while birds sing freedom to the sky;
cars pass, filled with people going somewhere,
not writing what comes.

i am chalk dust…
i am invisible…
a sponge…
once i too wore shorts
and Roman sandals…

Walt Whitman dreams he strolls naked
through a party, his genitals swinging,
while the chandeliers sparkle
on the shocked faces of the guests.
"I sing the body electric," he says.

They won't pick up my attendance sheets
because someone broke my clip.
I ask for a new one.
"Call Maintenance," they say,
then send me a note to tell me
I haven't turned in my sheets.

Outside, sprawled on the grass,
my students talk as they paint.
They don't want to come in.
Their canvases are thick and cracked,
but still, they add more coats.
They bend over the glorious days
while the birds sing freedom to the sky.
Sunlight shocks the young girls' faces
as they paint and sing
the body electric.

SHADES

Gauguin's woman reclines on a hot pink beach,
a wreath of white plumeria in her hair.
Through downcast eyes she gazes
at my pale pink bathroom—
the white countertop
crowded with makeup,
moisturizers, sunscreen.
Gazes at my pale pink body,
past childbearing years.

A brown Earth Goddess,
broad feet, broad hands, broad hips,
she belongs to the tropic sun.

Hot pink, the color of
passion, the color of
her full lips,
of the inside of mouths
of red insistent tongues,
the color of the inside of elbows,
of erect nipples,
of the hidden vulva—
entrance to the hot pink
home of pleasure,
of procreation.

IN THE SHADOW OF THE BALBOA PAVILION

My Grandson and I stand
in the shadow of the Balboa Pavilion
and watch the flow of traffic.
He is content as long as I
jiggle the hands of his stroller.
If I forget, his glance reminds me
that he, nearing two, is in his ascendancy,

while my star is in its decline.

There are many babies, many strollers,
for this is a sunny day in spring.
I stare at the woman who wears
two strips of metallic fabric
criss-crossed over her nipples.
I stare again at a bearded man
whose tattoos cover his body,
stopping at wrists and ankles like cuffs.
His ladyfriend has one rose tattooed above her heart.
Their Harley is parked at the curb.

The horn of the ferry argues its right-of-way.
Pinball machines clang, the barker chants
his come-on for the bay cruise.
Scents of popcorn, cotton candy,
mustard and salt air.
And underneath it all—
the stale smell of waste and diesel fuel.

This is not a day for newspapers
nor taxes nor rumors of wars.
Nor is it a day for meditations
on the brevity of existence.
This is a sunny day in spring.
There are smiles on the faces of the people.
Nature will continue her blind rebirth.
Leaves unfurl, poppies explode overnight.
Ants commence their building
and carrying away of crumbs.

TERRY B. STEVENSON

TERRY STEVENSON'S poems have appeared in *Poetry L.A.*, *ONTHEBUS*, *Voices*, *Blood Pudding*, *Electrum*, *Rattle*, *Spillway*, and *onTarget*. He has also been published in the anthologies, *Shards*, *Off-Ramp*, *Corners* (Pasadena Poets), *The New Los Angeles Poets* (Bombshelter Press), and *Truth and Lies that Press for Life* (Artifact Press). He is the Senior Assistant City Attorney for the City of Burbank. He lives in Sylmar with his wife, Mary, and eight-year-old son Devin.

GARY'S FRIEND

He never knew my name
one of us
had blanks in his rifle
but it wasn't me
I am a marksman
I take pride in the way
a rifle responds to my touch
I knew
when I squeezed the trigger
and watched the bullet leave the barrel
spiraling like a perfectly
thrown football
I followed the bullet's flight
into Gilmore's chest
straight into his heart

I thought of my ma and pa
taking me and my little brother
to see *Ol' Yeller*
the theater was so large
we sat in the balcony
pa got us coke and buttered popcorn
lots of paper napkins
for our fingers
that moment
when the kid
had to shoot his best friend
no choice
Ol' Yeller gone rabid
the kid walked away
bent from the weight
of becoming a man
I cried for days

Some jobs just have to be done
like putting down injured livestock
or shooting a rabid dog
I didn't like it much

but I've never lost any sleep over it
fact is
I remember it
as the best shot of my life.

BIRTH DAY

1: DEVIN

Thump
      thump
           bump
               bump
                   bump

                   squeeeeeeeezzzzeee
                     can't swim anymore

                    fall
                      fall
                        fall.

2: TERRY

The moment we checked
into the hospital
the contractions stopped.
We waited
and waited;
after about three hours
our OB induced labor.

I told Mary
to squeeze my hand
and she crushed it.
I pulled my hand away
and gave her a tennis ball.
She squeezed it tight
and then threw it at my head.

Two more hours
and my son's head crowned
I was standing behind the bed,
looked directly into his blue eyes,
watched as he took it all in,
very deliberate,
turned his head to look around the room.

And some doctors say
that babies can't see
for hours or days after birth.

3: MARY

"You're too old!"
That's what my 21 year old son said
when I told him I was pregnant.
I remember that this morning
as we go to the hospital.
My husband brings along some books
he thinks he is going to read
while he waits to be needed
to coach me.

After the pitocin
all I want are drugs
to stop the pain.
I push and push
and my OB and my husband
are talking about sports.
If I had a gun I'd kill
them both.

Then
all bloody and pink
he comes.
Fuzzy hair red like mine
eyes blue like his father's.

The doctor puts him
on my chest.
The cord still makes us one,
then it is cut.
And for the first time,
not the last time,
he is on his own.

Thump
        thump
                bump

all fall down.

MOWING THE LAWN

My dad never owned a power mower.
I mowed the lawn
with his cast-iron push mower.
I would fake sunstroke
in the hot LA summers
so my friends would finish
the sweaty chore.

My dad had a lot of tools.
He liked to build things,
use his hands.
This wisdom he passed on
to my younger brother,
but not to me.

My dad had jet black hair,
slicked back,
bright blue eyes,
and a strong chin.
The only thing I got from him
was the blue eyes.

My dad stands in front

of the Olvera Street nativity scene,
bleary and bewildered,
has no idea it's Baby Jesus in the manger.
He turns to my mom
and slurs, "Who's it?"

My dad walks alone from the dorm
at the Veteran's Hospital in Westwood.
He is being treated for all the symptoms.
I pick him up to take him
with me and my friends
to the beach.

We go surfing.
He goes to the supermarket at the corner
of Pacific Coast Highway and Sunset.
He must swill his Jim Beam
before we can take him back to the VA.

Today
I mow my lawn.
It is a typical May day
in the San Fernando Valley,
warm with high clouds
so thick the foothills disappear
in the mist.

I use a push mower.
Once I had a gardener do it.
Then Mary Riley gave me this push mower.
It's environmentally correct
and socially cool for exercise.
But after about fifteen minutes
I'm sweating and thinking of my dad,
the two shots of tequila I drank
before mowing the lawn,
the two more that I will have
when I finish—
and I know the wisdom
he passed to me.

ROOM 592

I must use the staff elevator
to the fifth floor.
Construction blocks the main elevator.
There are three staff elevators.
The one to the left arrives first.
I step in and notice a dent
in the linoleum floor
in the shape of a hoof print.

I wonder what a horse
would be doing in the staff elevator
at St. Joseph's Medical Center.
I am sure it would be a loyal horse
come to take his master home
or a gentle filly
here to nuzzle a sick child
to wakefulness.

If only I knew that compassion
I would squeeze it into an apple
bright as a heart and give it to my mother
who waits for me in room 592.
Me, only a son
who knows his mother has cancer.
Only a son,
not a loyal horse
to take her home,
to nuzzle her,
wake her up and tell her
not to worry,
it's only a nightmare.

LOSING TEETH

Devin is losing one of his lower front teeth.
The toddler who, with hardly a tear,

could take an eight-stitch gash
above the eyelid from falling headfirst
into the corner of the TV set,
has grown into a six-year-old
who is crying from the pain of an emerging tooth,
the loss of another.

I tell him that the Tooth Fairy will reward
those who are brave,
those who can handle the pain
having a body brings.
I show him the scar from the surgery
on my Achilles tendon,
ruptured going for a rebound.
He understands the scar.
He has reached that age
when he knows what it means
to take the body apart.

He goes to his room
and I walk into the kitchen.
I notice the paper plate
with his last meal, uneaten.
His mother had taken the time to cut
his turkey sandwich into dime-sized pieces,
carefully crushed the potato chips into small bits,
so that he could eat without pain.

THE COUGH

It is one of my earliest memories.
I could hear it backstage
in the auditorium
of Theodore Roosevelt Elementary School.
I knew exactly where she was sitting,
the exact seat.

A deep, long sound
like starting a car

on a cold morning
or a jackhammer ripping asphalt.
She would finally clear the tar
from her lungs and it would stop.

This afternoon, in the hospital,
I held my mom's hand
and listened for the cough again.

PRIORITIES

I am a mountain climber
who has lost his hold.
My only salvation
is the rope around my waist.
She has the rope.
I can't see her face.

She will save me
or let me slip away.
If she pulls me up
I will give her what
she wants;
my tongue between her thighs,
searching deep in her dampness,
finding just the right spot
licking until it grows—
stands erect easy to find.
I will not stop until
she floods my mouth
with her sweetest juice.

This will not be enough for her.
I am not really a mountain climber.
I am just a husband
whose wife has lost faith.
I iron my shirts
while I watch the football game.
She brings the laundry

in from the garage,
tells me how tired she is,
how she wishes she could do
the yardwork that needs to be done,
that it is her first priority.

PRAYERS

Tonight
as my son and I say his prayers
he stops at blessing his father.
No—
he tells me—
he won't do that.
He will bless his mother
but not me
because I yelled
at his mother.

I explain to him
I made a mistake,
lost my temper.
I look at his little face.
The darkness in his room
is broken by his Winnie-the-Pooh nightlight.
He will not hear my confession.
I have forever changed
his view of life.
Of me.
There is no forgiveness
in this night.

NO MEMORY

My mother's birthday
is next Thursday.
It is the first birthday
after her death.

I think about this
as my son and I say
his evening prayers:

"God bless my mother,
my father, my brother,
my uncles, my aunts,
my grandma Joan,
and my grandma who is in heaven."

I know that as he grows older
he will have no memory of my mother.
He will forget
her eyes were blue like his.
He will forget
her courage and her fear.
He will forget
how she tried to love him,
but could not get past
the distance between
herself and his mother.

He will not remember any of it.
He will see himself in video tapes
with my mother
but he won't remember the feel of her skin,
her smell, her smile and laugh,
the way he played with her oxygen tank,
pushing the red button that showed how much
oxygen was left before the tank was empty.

I don't remember
my great-grandmother,
the last Stuart.
I see myself in black-and-white photographs
sitting in her lap.
She was a large woman for her time,
standing over six foot tall.
But I don't remember sitting in her lap.
As far as I'm concerned

it never happened.

I will tell Devin the stories
of my mother's life.
How as a teenager she drove cars
from the San Fernando Valley
to Riverside for her father's
car dealership.
The World War II years,
working at North American
watching a mock dogfight
between a Lockheed P-38
and a Mustang P-51.
Rubbing elbows in the Fifties and Sixties
with movie and television stars,
how she tried to save my father
from alcoholism and failed.
The final years—
the heavy smoking,
the emphysema,
the cancer that killed her.

I had hoped
she would tell him her own story.
That last month
I left her a tape recorder
and asked her to tape something
for him.
I thought it would take her mind
off the end.
After she died
I found the tape recorder
on the table beside her bed.

There was nothing on the tape.

JEREMY STUART

JEREMY STUART was born in London but spent a large part of his childhood traveling. He has been living in California since 1985. After a ten-year love affair with music, he turned his interests to writing. His poetry has appeared in *ONTHEBUS, Voices, onTarget, Vol.No., Whoreson Dog* and *Spillway,* He has also published six chapbooks. He currently lives in Los Angeles where he works as a freelance video editor.

THE FEAST

We dock the light boat along the shoal
and swing our buckets onto the sand
brimming with salt water and fish,
some still thrashing that last dance before death.
The rusted anchor sinks and bites the sand
as we make our way to the dark wood tables
set for fishermen to prepare the day's catch.
My father is sloshing in his rubber boots,
his hands are around the rough tin handles
of the plastic pails, and water spills onto the grass.
The table stands wet and slippery in the sun
lined with iridescent fish scales and dried blood.
My father's friend, the fisherman, plunges his hands
into the slick and grapples a thrashing fish to the table top.
He pinches the jaw open with thumb and forefinger,
and rips the fishhook free from the bloodied lip.
I lean into the black and melancholy hole of the fish's eye,
as the knife severs the head in a single cut.
When I touch the body with my fingers, laying it to rest,
the fishtail curls and settles on the wood.
One long cut made with the tip of the blade
removes the guts and entrails.
Then the fisherman puts down his blade and turns,
his thumbs glistening with sequins
from the ritual undressing of the fish.
The fish sizzles in the pan with oil and garlic.
We sit around the dinner table at the camp
and wait for the feast,
wine in our glasses, water on the boil.
"Eat, eat," says the fisherman and passes me
a slice of the white meat
juice oozing onto the plate.
And we eat.
The three of us in silence.
Quiet and calm and grateful.

TURNING TO THE WORK

Back then I would have done anything for money.
I was broke, struggling, hungry for life,
and I tried it all.
From the fish market, to the lumberyard,
from the street-cleaning crews
with their brooms and pushbarrows,
the black sacks stuffed
into baggy overall pockets,
from the meat counter carcasses
stiff on butcher's hooks,
and the pungent aroma of cold blood,
to the mundane stacking of boxes at night
in the dank warehouse,
with its shadows and cobwebs,
and blinding dust.

I came home smelling of fish and grease,
vegetable oil, beef dripping,
my shoes thick with the dirt of the streets.
I came home with my hands yellowed
from wet paste, dry as cardboard,
cracking, calloused,
dotted with splinters,
wood chips, angry paint.
I came home with the faces
of my fellow workers fresh
in my mind.

Raymond, with his hands bent at the wrist,
fingers gnarled to hardened stumps from the presses.
The ink under his nails,
stamped into his skin like a tattoo.
John with his steel-capped boots
and blue slacks,
grappling with the fifty-gallon drums
that arrived all night at the chemical plant,

his face, powdered with chemicals, beaded with sweat,
hands gripped tight around the steel straps
of the loading bay trucks.
And Bill, his starched white shirts and greasy shoes,
arms patches of red welts from the splashing of the fat,
the great vats hissing, fish turning in the hot oil . . . .

It always comes back to this,
the work,
the turning to what lasts.
"Work hard," my father once said
"And you'll never go wrong."
"The work, it gets into your bones,
and you live on it."

THE GIFT

The kitchen air fills with the smell of rising dough.
My father stands over the ceramic bowl
working the mix.
Kneading the dough with his whitened knuckles,
he pounds it into the bowl
and then lifts it out to breathe.
His greased hands swell like yeast
as he folds the dough,
parting it into equal thirds—
one loaf for him,
one for my mother,
and, for my sister and me,
six small rolls
rising like ripe breasts
under a damp dishcloth.

He greases the tins,
then washes his hands in the sink.
The grey light gathers in the eaves.

It is Sunday evening.
Soon, when the light disappears,
he will place the tins in the oven.
The bread will rise
and take on its honey-colored glow.
We will gather in the kitchen
like baby birds,
greedy mouths upon the bread.
For this is my father's gift.
This simple gift of bread and salt.
The wealth of melting butter.
A warm loaf pressed against the chest.

STRANGERS

By the time I awoke, we were in the air
and already well on the way
to the islands of Southern Thailand.
She sat beside me,
her head resting on my shoulder,
this dark-haired angel,
a complete stranger I had met
two days previous in the market.
She was broke
and needed a ride South
so I paid for her ticket.
We went in style
as if we were lovers on a honeymoon.
I asked for nothing in return
save for her company
on the long dark night
when the sun had fallen behind the hills
and the water lay motionless and heavy
in the moonlight.
That night she lay by my side
in the Eight-by-Six room

as if I were a long lost friend.
Her body warm and supple
against my back
breathing into me.
I didn't tell her of my life.
It seemed safer to remain strangers
sharing only the moments as they arose,
knowing that in the morning she would be gone
leaving me with all I have of her now.
Her name.
The sound of her voice.
Her warm
gracious
smile.

DRIVING HOME

It was sixty-five miles home to London
from the stormy coast,
with its stone beaches
and weather-beaten promenade,
the turquoise paint peeling
from wrought iron rails
that lined the boardwalk.

Dad at the wheel
navigating the road
in the dark.
Eyes squinting
against the oncoming headlights,
leaning forward
as we entered the curves.

My mother, next to him,
a poised mouse,
her hands like careful shovels
folded upon her lap.

How many evenings spent alone
waiting up for him?
His staggering hulk
barging through the door,
all slurs and regrets.

I knew then it would not last.
I knew by the way she looked at him
from the corner of her eye,
by the way the streetlights
caught her frozen stare,
by his wrinkled brow,
and by their silence,
saying all that needed to be said.

And my young sister,
too small to know,
curled beside me in the backseat,
the curves of the road
rocking her sleep,
deepening her dreams.

HOW I WRITE A POEM

First, I wash the breakfast dishes.
Carefully dry each piece of cutlery
so the water stains won't remain
on the hollow curve of a spoon,
or the blade of a knife.
Then I brush my teeth,
examining the gaps between them
or practice making faces
to suit my mood that day,
lifting the corners of my mouth
into a grin, or pulling a frown.

I dry my hands

and pad into the bedroom
in search of my shoes.
Calling out the twin syllable
of my dog's name,
whose trained ears
recognize the sound
I make as I drop
to one knee to put my shoes on.

During our walk around the block,
I fiddle with a smooth rock
I carry in my right pocket.
Walking to the beat of iambs,
I am wide-eyed like Picasso,
strolling the forests of Fontainebleau,
overwhelmed by the "Indigestion of greenness"
around him,
wanting to remember everything,
every curled leaf and fallen acorn,
each footstep left behind
from a previous day.

I take the same route home.
My dog follows close on my heels.
And poetry? Ah poetry,
well, first I wash the breakfast dishes,
I walk my dog around the block
and take the same route,
the same route home.

BARBER SHOP

My father bows his head
into the sink
and the barber holds the weight in one hand
like a newborn child,
pours water from a jug with the other.

My father's head in this strange man's hands,
a ritual among men.

Then, his head comes up,
water rolls down his cheeks,
the towel is draped around his shoulders,
and the creamy white foam
on the stiff bristles of a fox hair brush,
paint my father's cheeks and chin:
an old man
with a distinguished white beard
as I imagined he would be in forty years.

The barber steps on a bar
to raise the chair, and reaches for his tools
with the precision of a surgeon.
He begins with the razor,
unsheathed from its pocket
of worn brown leather.
His focused eye and steady hand
trace the contours of the face,
chin held aloft on three fingers
as if holding up a prize.

EDIBLE

Ask me what I am
and I point to fruit.
Fruit packed in crates
upon the grocer's table.
I am the drool upon the chin,
the sweet nectar of peaches
or pears,
and oh for the love of seeds
between the teeth.
Pulp to be rolled around the tongue
and sucked pips spat high
into the expectant air.

I am nectarines and plums,
I am peeled grapes
without skin or bones,
marrow only marrow to the core.

Ask me what I am
and I sing the music
of honey dripping on a fig leaf.
Sugar lips and candy fingers
wrapped around lobes of kumquat,
oils of mango.
Wrinkled skin upon a prune,
oranges crushed by crimson skies.
Tangerines and junipers,
all wetness and berries.
I am loam and I am peat,
I am moss on a tree limb,
fur on the lip of a peach.

Blood on your fingers.
Sticky and raw.
Red and ripe.
Ready to be eaten.

AT THE END OF AMERICA

When I look up,
I can see the lights of the ferryboats
crossing the Strait of San Juan De Fuca.
I can see the end of America,
Canada in the distant north.
It is late in the evening,
and there is still no moon.
This far north, the days stretch longer
than I can extend the length of my darkness.
I take to looking up for a sense of comfort,
the kind found only in a sky
riddled with pockets of light;

light that has traveled a great distance
to be seen, is light to be treasured,
it is light to be held against the breast
like a jewel.

At a quarter to ten, I am ready
to turn in.
I gather my things from the grass—
my pens, my paper,
an empty cup,
and when I look back across the water,
the moon has begun to rise
out of the torn horizon.
The light gathers in the trees
throwing shadows together like old friends.
The waves begin their song of erosion.
How can I love what fades,
when the wind breathes life into everything,
and the moon stretches its thin fingers
across the bay,
and reaches for my feet?

THE BLACK CAT

Imagine the poor repairman,
as he crawled on his belly
in the tight space under the house,
flashlight in one hand, a wrench in the other
to fix the broken pipe,
and came face to face
with that rotting ball
of stiff black hair and dusty bones,
the black cat
dead for three months now,
maybe more.

I've no idea how he got there.
Once, I saw him dash under the house
through a hole in the crawlspace.
I flushed him out with a broom
and then sealed the hole with a few old bricks.
I thought he was gone.
I had no idea I was sealing a tomb,
stacking up bricks to trap him
in the cool underbelly of this old house.

Imagine, my wife and I sleeping at night in peace.
Happy in our house,
and dreaming for our lives
unaware of the struggle beneath us.
That quiet battle with death.
And the cat listening to our creaking footsteps,
mumbled voices.
All the pipes hissing as they carried our water away,
and, with his belly to the earth,
the black cat lay parched
licking the dust.
Not even strong enough
to raise his voice.